Hybrid Warfare and its Impact on Pakistan's Security

SAGHIR IQBAL

ISBN-10: 1721510095
ISBN-13: 978-1721510092

DEDICATION

I dedicate this book to all those who gave me encouragement, support and guidance. Foremost, to my father (late) Raja Mohammed Iqbal and to my mother Azra Begum, from whom I have learnt so much. In addition to my wife Neghat Khan, who was patient and extremely helpful in my trying times. Furthermore, to Raja Nasser Razak Khan, Raja Nadeem Arif, Raja Hamza Ali, Raja Umaire Ali, Raja Usama Tahir, Husnaa Tahir, Neelam Rauf, Hafsa Iqbal, Zainab Iqbal. And finally I dedicate this to my three colleagues – Mohammed Rafiq, Tahir Bashir and Fiaz Ahmed.

CONTENTS

ACKNOWLEDGMENTS

I am very grateful to a host of people for their various contributions towards this book. I am particularly very grateful to Professor Syed Peerzada Mahmud Shah Bookhari who deserves much commendation for his constant encouragement and support throughout the hard times of the programme.

Hybrid Warfare and its Impact on Pakistan's Security

Abstract

The global security challenges after the post-Cold war period has affected many countries. Pakistan has particularly been affected with many issues, primarily its war on terror. Pakistan faces a multitude number of threats from internal and external forces – with the aim of weakening the country and an attempt to 'balkanise' Pakistan in to different parts. Pakistan has been dismembered in the past by India (1971 war) when it lost East Pakistan to become Bangladesh. There is widespread evidence to suggest that similar attempts are being made by Pakistan's enemies to further weaken and split the country. It is argued by many that Pakistan's adversaries are successfully operating the various hybrid warfare methods to 'bleed' the country. Due to the inability of these foreign powers to coerce Pakistan with their conventional and nuclear arsenals – they have chosen the hybrid warfare route. Pakistan's enemies are making alliances and devising new trade routes in order to isolate Pakistan and robustly continue to propagate sophisticated propaganda against it. In order to damage the countries stability, various attempts have been made to finance militants - with the overall aim of causing widespread instability via terrorist activities.

This book will be assessing Pakistan's insecurity and the hybrid wars imposed onto it by its adversaries. It will look at a number of issues that Pakistan is facing (military imbalance, economic and political weaknesses, internal and external security threats and the impact of hybrid warfare on Pakistan).

PAF Air space monitoring

Abbreviation

ASCM – Ani-ship Cruise Missile

AAR - Air to air refuelling

APC – Armoured Personal Carrier

AEW&C – Airborne Early Warning and Control Aircraft

ALCM/GLCM – Air Launched Cruise Missile/ Ground Launched Cruise Missile

AWACS – Airborne Warning and Control System

BMD – Ballistic Missile Defence

BVR – Beyond Visual Range (air-air-missile)

CSD – Cold Start Doctrine

ICBM – Intercontinental Ballistic Missile

IAF – Indian Air Force

IN – Indian Navy

JF-17 – Joint Fighter 17 Thunder (Pakistani derivative)

MBT – Main Battle Tank

NCWF – New Concept of War Fighting

PAC – Pakistan Aeronautical Complex

PAF – Pakistan Air Force

PN – Pakistan Navy

PGM - Precision guided munitions (Smart weapons)

SAM – Surface to Air Missile

SLCM – Submarine Launched Cruise Missile

UCAV – Unmanned Combat Aerial Vehicle

US Apache Gunship helicopter

Chapter 1: Hybrid Warfare

Pakistan Army special forces (SSG) Troops on national parade day

"War is not an independent phenomenon, but the continuation of politics by different means".

- Carl von Clausewitz

Conflicts and warfare have changed due to the technological innovations that have been developed in different eras. Warfare has been given different names due to these changes and in an historical context have been used in different eras when the opportunity arose. A brief look at the different warfare by stages is as follows:

First-generation warfare	This primarily refers to the earliest stages of war that has been waged by organised by the armed forces of nations. Battles were fought by large armies (uniformed soldiers), using line and column tactics (wars of Napoleon, conscription and firearms).[1]
Second-generation warfare	With the development of new technological innovations, such as the invention of the rifled musket, breech-loading weapons, machine guns etc., the tactics of warfare had

---

[1] Global Guerrillas 4GW – Fourth Generation Warfare
http://globalguerrillas.typepad.com/globalguerrillas/2004/05/4gw_fourth_gene.html

	changed (World War 1, firepower and nation-state alignment of resources to warfare).
Third-generation warfare	Tactics were changed as technology increased – speed and surprise were used to bypass the enemy's lines and attack their forces from the rear until the enemy forces had capitulated. Line and column tactics where soldiers were meeting the opponents on an face to face basis was changing in to outmanoeuvring each other to gain a better position to inflict serious losses (World War 2, maneuver and armored warfare).
Fourth-generation warfare	This stage, with the Revolution in Military Affairs (rapid development of war related technology) had resulted in countries monopoly on military forces (combat) being reduced due to organised non-state actors. This warfare is viewed by the blurring lines between war and politics, soldier and civilian. In some cases it has been seen as the modes of conflict that was common in pre-modern times.[2]

According to Carl von Clausewitz (Prussian general and military theorist), **"Every age has its own kind of war, its own limiting conditions, and its own peculiar preconceptions"**.

Analysts are conjuring up new warfare terminology, such as 5th generation or Hybrid threats/wars etc. all to define a new era in warfare. However this has been criticised by many as nothing more than giving new fanciful names to different types of warfare that have been practiced in different scenarios and scale. Fourth-generation warfare theory and Hybrid warfare has been criticized on the grounds that it is "nothing more than repackaging of the traditional clash between the non-state insurgent and the soldiers of a nation-state.

Hybrid Warfare

A form of warfare evolved from 4th generation war that uses a number of strategies and techniques on an adversary to either to destroy or dismantle and make it a lot weaker. It uses political warfare, conventional and unconventional warfare, Information and Cyber Warfare, supporting local unrest, mass propaganda (Fake news websites etc.), diplomacy, intervention in foreign elections. Essentially any available technique of opportunity where the aggressor intends to avoid attribution or retribution.

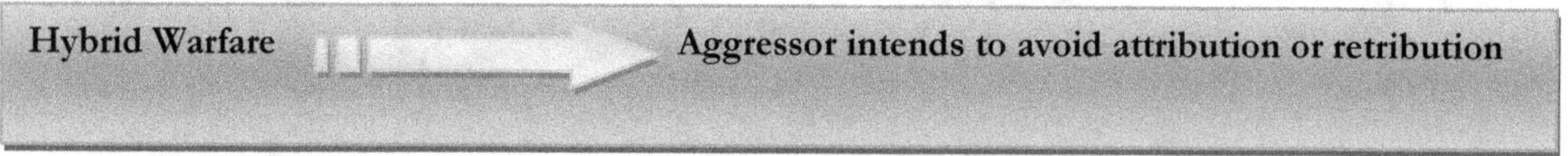

Hybrid warfare combines kinetic operations with destabilising efforts and aims to avoid attribution or retribution.[3]

Hybrid warfare Concept[4]

---

[2] Lind, William et al. (1989). The Changing Face of War: Into the Fourth Generation.
https://www.mcamarines.org/files/The%20Changing%20Face%20of%20War%20%20Into%20the%20Fourth%20Generation.pdf

[3] Reid Standish (2018) Inside a European Center to Combat Russia's Hybrid Warfare -
https://foreignpolicy.com/2018/01/18/inside-a-european-center-to-combat-russias-hybrid-warfare/

[4] Hybrid Warfare: Briefing to the Subcommittee on Terrorism, Unconventional Threats and Capabilities, Committee on Armed Services, House of Representatives (September 10, 2010) - https://www.gao.gov/assets/100/97053.pdf

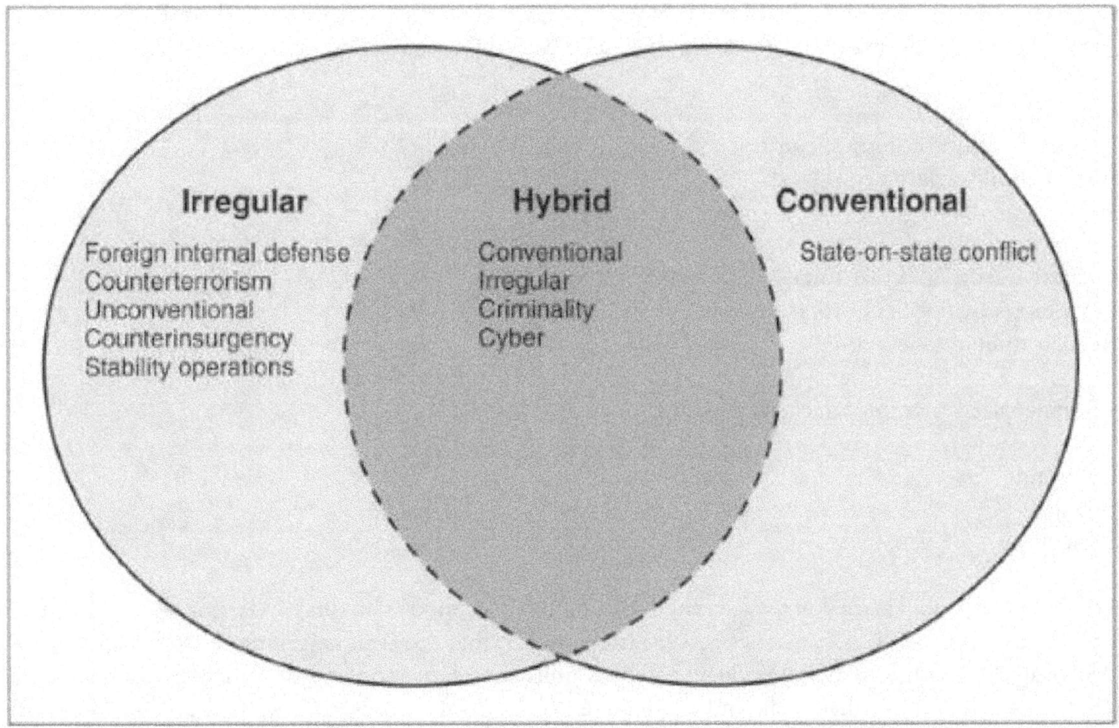

Conflicts in Ukraine, Israel and Lebanon (Hizbullah), Syria, Libya, War on Terror in Afghanistan and its impact in Pakistan etc., have resulted in multi-layered efforts to destabilise a functioning state and polarize its society. The centre of gravity is to target population in hybrid warfare. The aim of the adversary is to influence influential policy makers and key decision makers by combining kinetic operations with subversive efforts. The aggressor often resorts to covert actions, to avoid attribution or retribution.[5]

At the moment there is no universally accepted definition of hybrid wars – the term is too abstract and is seen by some as using a fancy term to refer to irregular methods to counter conventionally stronger forces. Accordingly, many say that the new definitions of 4th generation or hybrid wars are really the repackaging of the traditional clash between the armed forces of nation states and the non-state insurgents.

According to the academic Anam Sheikh, **"Hybrid warfare is all about engaging the enemy in all types of warfare from all the fronts simultaneously. The threats are multiple ranging from conventional, non-conventional and irregular. Hybrid warfare is a form of fourth generation warfare that is more decentralized, fluid and asymmetrical in its nature. One can say that hybrid warfare is a supreme tactic that is designed to target adversary's opportunity of growth without waging a real war".[6]**

Pakistan faces a multitude number of threats from internal and external forces – with the aim of weakening the country and an attempt to balkanise Pakistan in to different parts. The Pakistani Chief of Army, General Qamar Javed Bajwa said a **"hybrid war had been imposed on Pakistan to internally weaken it, but noted that the enemies were failing to divide the country on the basis of ethnicity and other identities"**. Furthermore he states, **"Our**

---

[5] Deterring hybrid warfare: a chance for NATO and the EU to work together? https://www.nato.int/docu/review/2014/Also-in-2014/Deterring-hybrid-warfare/EN/index.htm

[6] Anam Sheikh (2017), India's hybrid warfare in Pakistan - https://www.globalvillagespace.com/indias-hybrid-warfare-in-pakistan/

enemies know that they cannot beat us fair and square and have thus subjected us to a cruel, evil and protracted hybrid war. They are trying to weaken our resolve by weakening us from within".[7]

According to the writer and analyst Dr Farrukh Saleem, a Hybrid war has been imposed on Pakistan. He states that Pakistan is under an eight dimensional attack that has been waged under various strategies as follows:

(1) Economic warfare;
(2) Foreign support of domestic unrest
(3) Information warfare propaganda
(4) Diplomatic onslaught
(5) Cyber attacks
(6) Offensive from irregular forces
(7) Operations by Special Forces
(8) Regular military operations.[8]

There are 3 dimensions that this attack is based on:

(1) Economic
(2) Political
(3) Societal.

The aim of Pakistan's adversaries are to weaken the nation's economy so that it is unable to allocate adequate resources for its defence needs. A constant pressure is exerted so that the country continues to borrow money and get into the debt-trap. Hence International trade and debt is utilised as a weapon of war. Furthermore, weak and corrupt governments are supported so that weak and ineffective governments are used to keep the progress of the country down. It is argued that weak governments are more prone to incorporate unsound economic projects that will further cause economic instability in the country. In addition, weaknesses in Pakistan's society are being exploited to cause further unrest/divisions and possible desire of splitting the country (as was in the case of Pakistan being dismembered by India's support for disgruntled groups in the past when it lost the former East Pakistan to Bangladesh). There are widespread evidence that the attempt to further dismember Pakistan has been implanted by a number of countries such as the USA and India (with the support and help of their respective allies).[9]

The writer and analyst Andrew Korybko further states that the Hybrid War on Pakistan has been intensified by countries such as the USA to damage its International relations and standing. He gives the following opinion, **"it can be expected that the US and its global Mainstream Media partners will reframe everything in the reverse by making the world think that the Pakistani victims are really the aggressors and that the Americans are completely innocent of any wrongdoing".** [10] It is argued that Pakistan's adversaries are successfully operating the various hybrid warfare methods to 'bleed' the country. Due to the inability of these foreign powers to coerce Pakistan with their conventional and nuclear arsenals – they have chosen the hybrid warfare route. Pakistan's enemies are making alliances and devising new trade routes in order to isolate Pakistan and robustly continue to propagate sophisticated propaganda against it and also finance militants to cause widespread instability and terrorist activities to further damage the country's stability.[11] We will look at Pakistan's security issues and the implications of Hybrid Warfare on this nation.

---

[7] 'Hybrid war' imposed on country to internally weaken it, says Bajwa (15 April 2018), https://www.dawn.com/news/1401747

[8] Pakistan under hybrid war attack from eight dimensions (2018) https://timesofislamabad.com/22-Apr-2018/pakistan-under-hybrid-war-attack-from-eight-dimensions

[9] Ibid.

[10] Andrew Korybko (2018), Pakistan And America Are In The Throes Of A Serious Diplomatic Crisis: https://orientalreview.org/2018/05/19/pakistan-and-america-are-in-the-throes-of-a-serious-diplomatic-crisis/

[11] Dr Zafar Nawaz Jaspal (Associate Professor, School of Politics and International Relations), Hybrid warfare's menace (2017) https://pakobserver.net/hybrid-warfares-menace

Chapter 2: Pakistan's Security Issues

Pakistan's geography and location present its security planners with serious, almost irresolvable strategic and tactical problems. It borders the nuclear states of India and China, an ambitious Iran, and an unstable Afghanistan, which is perceived as a gateway to its commercial-strategic ambitions in Central Asia. Pakistan's key security problems are a reflection of its history and domestic circumstances. Located in a critical and historically contentious part of the world, Pakistan was composed of two wings, East Pakistan (renamed Bangladesh when it became independent in the 1971 war with India) and West Pakistan from its birth in 1947.[12]

The overriding concern of Pakistan is its internal and external security. Strategically, Pakistan lacks territorial depth. Its main cities and communication routes are relatively close to the border with India and are susceptible to attack. In addition, the headwater of Pakistan's rivers and main irrigation systems originate from India. Pakistan's borders with India were also new and mainly unfortified and, in many places, were drawn in ways that made them indefensible. Because the borders were also un-demarcated, there was abundant chance for conflict.[13]

Pakistan Map[14]

According to Pakistan, its major threats continue to arise from the immediate neighbourhood. Of utmost concern is the Indian threat and the status of Kashmir (the K in Pakistan's name). Since independence in 1947 Indian and Pakistan have gone to war three

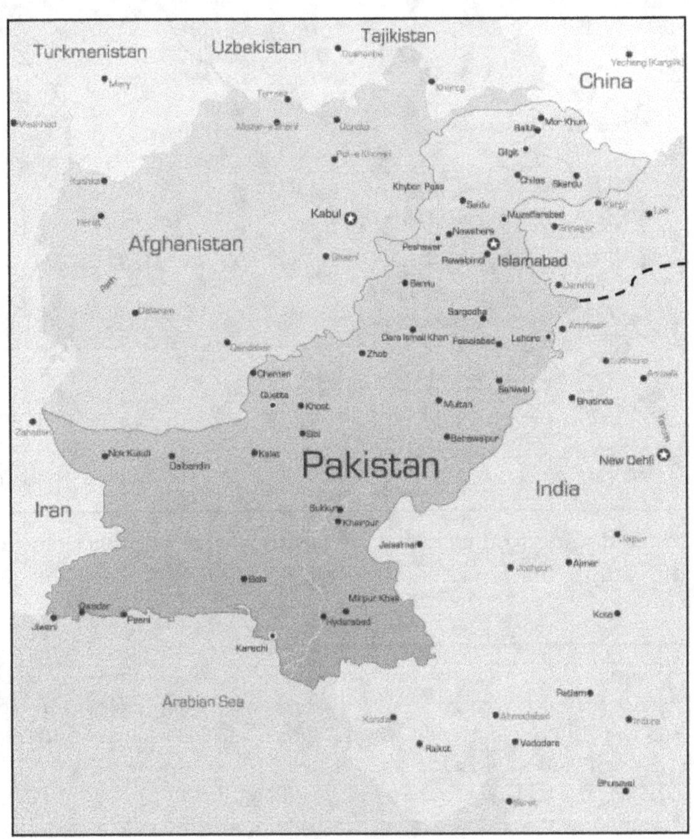

---

[12] Hafeez Malik, Dilemmas of National Security and Co-operation, The Macmillan Press Ltd, 1993, Pg1
[13] Mustaq Ali Khan, Pakistan Army Green Book, Ferozsons (Pvt) Ltd, 1990, Pg292
[14] http://www.beautifulholidays.com.au/travel-guide/asia/pakistan/index.php

times,[15] conducted hundreds of other skirmishes and artillery exchanges, and have assisted separatist movements in each other's countries, primarily over the territorial issue of Kashmir.[16] Moreover this root cause between them has not only remained unresolved, but it is as hot and volatile as ever before. Both countries have nuclear weapons and if their bad neighbourly relations flare up any more, there is a serious risk that nuclear war could break out. India and Pakistan each claim that their nuclear weapons are intended to deter the other, but neither has ruled out the first use of these weapons.[17]

Both nations possess advanced military aircraft that would be capable of delivering nuclear weapons.[18] Of greater concern, because of their speed and invulnerability to conventional air-defence systems, are both nations' ballistic missiles. [19] Reports in 1997 indicated that India has possibly deployed, or at least was storing, conventionally armed Prithvi missiles in Punjab, very near the Pakistani border. These missiles reduce warning time on both sides to nearly zero, making any nuclear crisis extremely unstable. India and Pakistan could hit targets in each other's countries in less than three minutes.[20]

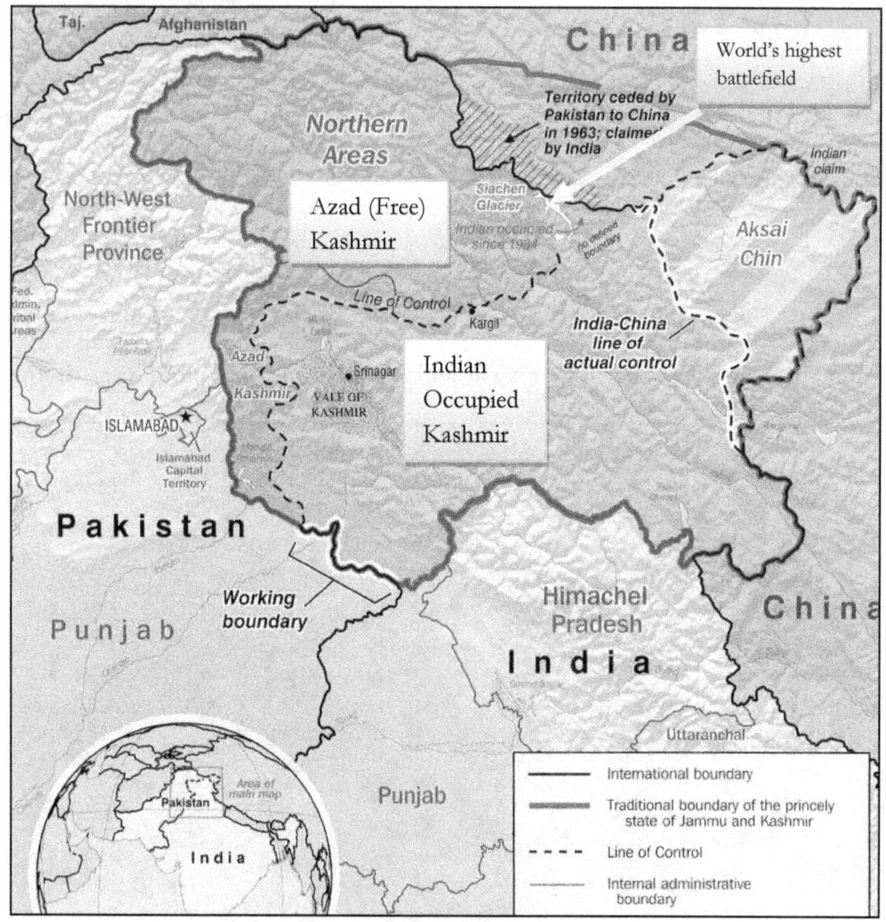

Disputed Area of Kashmir Map[21]

Although Pakistan perceived in India a threat to its security, initially it was not able to defend itself against that perceived threats because of limited personnel and material. In terms of all other key measurements such as size, population, resources, and general military strength, India holds an overwhelming advantage.[22] Pakistan therefore chose to develop a comprehensive military strategy that would offset at least some of its weaknesses. High hopes were placed on support from other Muslim nations, some of which could help financially and others of which would provide through alliances some of the geo-strategic territorial depth that Pakistan lacked.[23]

For Pakistan, strength was acquired by cultivating allies such as the United States and China, capitalising on its geographic position as an historic route to the sea for the Central Asian republics, and trying to use its Islamic credentials to gain allies.[24] With the end of the Soviet intervention in Afghanistan and the subsequent imposition of U.S. sanctions of Pakistan for

---

[15] Venon Hewit, The New International Politics of South Asia, Manchester University Press, 1997, Pg20

[16] Janes Defence Weekly (JDW), On the Line of Fire, Janes Information Group Ltd, 1998, Pg25

[17] David Albright and Tom Zamora, Indian and Pakistan go Nuclear, Bulletin of Atomic Scientists, 1989, Pg20

[18] Albright and Zamora, op cit:26

[19] JDW, Asia's Missile Race Hots Up, 1994m, Pg20

[20] Tarun Basu, Selective Sattelite Tracking of Missiles Alledged, India Abroad, 1997, Pg12

[21] http://legacy.lib.utexas.edu/maps/middle_east_and_asia/kashmir_disputed_2002.jpg

[22] Peter G. Tsourus, Changing Orders-The Evolution of the World's Armies, Arms and Armour Press, 1994, Pg 59

[23] Malik, op cit:133

[24] Malik, op cit:134

developing nuclear weapons,[25] Pakistan began to entertain hopes for establishing a strategic Islamic bloc consisting of Pakistan, Iran, Turkey, Afghanistan, and some of the new Central Asian Republics to stand against U.S. pressure and to protect itself against the effects of a U.S. tilt towards India.[26]

Pakistan's other security concern was over the ongoing conflict in neighbouring Afghanistan, which if not dealt with could undermine Pakistan's security and stability. Almost all of Pakistan's ethnic groups extend into neighbouring countries. This situation has caused problems with Afghanistan in the past, who did not recognise the border as valid and hoped that its new neighbour would be unable to assert its interests.[27]

Over three decades of war in Afghanistan has posed a dilemma for Pakistan's security, who has attempted to restrain the war in Afghanistan whilst also acting as a supply channel for material assistance from the West (mainly the US) and Arab countries. The influx of five million Afghan refugees in the past three decades has led to increasing levels of violence within Pakistan itself, including over twelve hundred bomb blasts, and an almost ubiquitous Kalashnikov and drug smuggling culture. America utilised Pakistan to settle scored with Soviet Union, but watered down relations after the end of the Soviet occupation.[28]

(L-R) President Ram Nath Kovind, his Iranian counterpart Hassan Rouhani and Prime Minister Narendra Modi in New Delhi.

Pakistan is also looking for commercial development opportunities, but its major prospect for commercial growth lie in opening a trade route to Central Asia, accessible via Afghanistan. In seeking to become Central Asia's conduit to the world, Pakistan is entering into direct competition with Iran, which is also seeking this role. At the same time, Pakistan has long hoped to develop closer relations with other Islamic states, including Iran. Pakistan's ties with Iran, following the Taliban's triumphant territorial gains in north Afghanistan and the murder of Iranian diplomats at Mazar-e-Sharif, are currently at their lowest. A near war situation prevailed on the Iran-Afghanistan border with increasing border clashes by both sides, when the Taliban were in power.[29] Iranian and Pakistani relationships have usually gone up and down during the past few centuries. Border tensions due primarily to smugglers and incidence of terrorism resulted in exchange of fire and mortars, killing security personnel on both sides. The Indian access to the Iranian Chahbahar port had further caused tensions,[30] when Indian Naval officer (that came through Iran) was caught in terrorist activities in Pakistan. Furthermore, an Iranian drone that was spying deep in Pakistan's restive Baluchistan province was shot down by the Pakistan Air Force (PAF).

Pakistan's external threat is enhanced by its internal problems, which are gradually assuming proportions that threaten its very survival as a nation. Pakistan's greatest problems are its political immaturity, which in turn has led to economic mismanagement, poor law and order, corruption, and ethnic and sectarian conflict. These conditions have cast a long and often destructive shadow on every nation-building activity in the country, hampering its economic prosperity and progress, and in turn impacting upon its defence capabilities.[31]

---

[25] Malik, op cit: 141

[26] JDW, op Country Survey-Pakistan, 1992, Pg 31

[27] JDW, op cit:30

[28] Ibid

[29] JDW, Will Iran Choose War?, 1998, Pg 23

[30] India, Iran discuss Pakistan, agree to lease Chabahar port to New Delhi - https://www.indiatoday.in/mail-today/story/india-s-diplomatic-strike-with-iran-in-chabahar-pakistan-terror-discussed-1172003-2018-02-18

[31] JDW, Mounting Tensions in South Asia, 1996, Pg57

The growing violence in Karachi is one example of an increasing proliferation of arms in Pakistan. As a result of arming the Mujahideen in Afghanistan, Pakistan faces an internal crisis with leftover arms from the Afghani war. Thus, Pakistan's future domestic tranquillity remains hostage in many ways to the continuation of the warfare in Afghanistan. Drugs and arms running and armed-gang attacks in the big cities are persisting manifestations of the Afghan war aftermath. Pakistan also faces the problem of religious extremism, with sectarian violence becoming common between Pakistan's Muslim Sunni majority and its Shia's minority.[32] Since Pakistan's recent anti-terrorism crackdown, things have started to get better.

Economic factors have also added to the nation's divisiveness. Prior to independence, Pakistan's localities were primarily based on rural economies, with most of the wealth and land held by a few families operating under a feudalistic system. Since independence these elite have continued to hold the reins of political power and have enjoy disproportional benefits from their status.[33]

Pakistan's vision is to portray itself as a moderate Islamic state as a buffer against extremist Iran, chaos in Afghanistan and uncertainty in Central Asia. However, the rise of religious fundamentalist influences in recent years, particularly the growth of Hindu fundamentalism in India symbolised by the popularity of the militant Bharatiya Janata Party **(BJP),** have greatly heightened tensions. Kashmir and Afghanistan are also a continuous problem, and internal social unrest has been blamed on outside factors, continuing the threat to Pakistan's security.[34]

Mi-35 Hind Gunship helicopter[35]

---

[32] Ibid
[33] B.H. Farmer, An Introduction to South Asia, Richard Clay & Co.Ltd, 1983, Pg211
[34] JDW, A Loss of Momentum, 1997, Pg 41
[35] https://pixabay.com/en/helicopter-free-military-helicopter-2198359/

Chapter 3: Pakistan's Key Threat Perceptions

Pakistan's military exercise

Pakistan's Threat Perceptions

As mentioned earlier, Pakistan and India have fought three major wars and various other confrontations since 1947. With Pakistan possessing only one-fourth of the land mass and less than one-sixth of the population of India, there are real concerns amongst Pakistani strategists that India could dismember their country in much the same way as in the 1971 war (a 'soft spot' would be through the Sindh province, separating the capital at Islamabad from the economic centre at Karachi) and defeat Pakistan's conventional forces in about two weeks.[36] The primary threat to its security if from India, and this section will look at this in detail.

The Military Imbalance

Pakistani strategies believe India's large army is well out of proportion to her defence needs. In particular, India's drive to modernise its army with well-equipped air and naval components, has significantly enhanced its power projection capabilities.[37] Relationship with China had, until recently, improved considerably. India's other neighbours are considered to be insignificant to pose any real threat. India's 20 year modernisation drive has enabled it to acquire a nuclear and ballistic missile capability, as well as improve its conventional military might. It has also greatly enhanced its strategic surveillance and reconnaissance abilities, with its own satellite with highly accurate imagery.[38] India's quest for great power status rather than national security is apparently uppermost in the minds of her politicians. We will look briefly at this conventional military capability, as well as that of Pakistan.

---

[36] JDW, Pakistan's time for Reassessment, 1988, Pg9
[37] 2.) Anthony H. Cordesman, Western Strategic Interests and the India-Pakistan Military Balance, Ian Allan Ltd, 1988, Pg83
[38] 3.) India Today, India is now a Nuclear Weapons State, Living Media India Ltd, 1998, Pg23

India has fought 3 major wars with Pakistan, and is currently engaged in a mini-war in the Siachin Glacier (Kashmir),[39] on the highest battlefield of the world. Recently, it has publicly demonstrated its designs on globally projecting its power. On at least two occasions, (in 1987 during India's Brasstacks' military exercise, and in the uprising in Kashmir in 1990), Kargil Mini-war in 1999, Pakistan and India have come close to full-scale military conflict.[40]

India's strategic (ICBM) nuclear capable ballistic missile on parade

Of particular concern for Pakistan is the open-source estimates that India has now manufactured between 95-100 nuclear devices.[41] In addition, the recent BJP government has been engaged in an open display of 'sabre-rattling' against Pakistan. It has openly declared its intention to 'take back' Pakistan-held Kashmir, as well as targeting of Pakistani cities, infrastructure, industries and defence installations by the Indian Air Force (IAF), and the development of new missile systems. These include the short range ballistic missile (SRBM) Prithvi and the intermediate range ballistic missile (IRBM) Agni; two surface to air missiles (SAM), the Trishul and the Akash; and also an anti-tank guided missile (ATGM), the Nag.[42] It has further tested Submarine Launched Ballistic Missiles from the Indian Submarine Arihant and has tested the Agni 5 Intercontinental Ballistic Missile (ICBM) with over 5,000 km range.

The Prithvi missile (150-350 km) and the development of the Agni IRBM (1500-2500 km) and other longer range series of Indian ballistic missiles provide India with the capability of targeting major Pakistani cities.[43] The plans to develop and deploy these missiles are seen by Pakistan as a proof of India's hostile designs. In addition, the procurement of 250 state-of-the-art Su-30MKI Flanker multi-role strike aircraft gives more punch to the Indian offensive capabilities on land and in the air, seriously undermining Pakistan's immediate and perceived security.[44]

---

[39] JDW, Fighting on the Roof of the World, 1998, Pg27

[40] India Today, Games of Brinkmanship, 1987, Pg8

[41] JDW, Trials Provide Data for Range of Weapons Yields, 1998, Pg3

[42] JDW, Asia's Missile Race Hots Up, 1994, Pg20

[43] Ibid

[44] JDW, IAF Follows up on SU-30 Offer, 1994, Pg4

Indian development and purchase of sophisticated weapons of all categories

India also has indigenous defence production programmes, including the manufacture of Soviet designed Mig-27 and British 'Jaguar' attack aircraft's the development of its own jet fighter that was initially called the light combat aircraft (LCA) is now known as Tejas and also an airborne warning and control (AWACS) aircraft. T-90/T-72 tanks, the design and manufacture of the 'Arjun' main battle tank (MBT), modern destroyers; frigates, missile boats, radar, command and communication systems and a full range of missiles and munitions are also in or past the development stages.[45]

---

[45] Impact International, Delhi Expands its Strategic Swath, News & Media Ltd, 1996, Pg24

India displays its military might during the Republic Day parade.

India is also purchasing various types of equipment from abroad, such as the planned purchase of over 1025+ advanced Russian T-90S Tanks with licenced production.[46] In addition, it is also planning to purchase over 600 self-propelled Howitzers for the Army,[47] over 100 combat capable trainers for the airforce,[48] the Admiral Gorshkov aircraft carrier from Russia. Its massive military build-up in the past two decades has been fully supported by India's indigenous defence manufacturing industries, enabling India to sustain a full scale conventional military conflict for a longer period if the need arose.[49]

Defence Budget and Arms Purchases

The India and Pakistan dispute has encouraged military modernisation in the region- the two countries are spending more on their military forces, making this part of the world the one region where military expenditure has been rising since the end of the Cold War. In the period from 1987-96 the two countries military expenditure had amounted to a massive $108.92 billion.[50] Since then it has increased massively, India alone intends to spend over $200 billion on defence systems by 2022.[51] The South Asian share of world military expenditure has increased over the past number of years, defence expenditures in 2017 amounted to some $62.22 billion ($52.5 billion for India and $9.72 billion Pakistan) and this was projected to rise every year.[52] As a percentage of their Gross Domestic Product (GDP), Pakistan spends a lot more on military expenditure as a percentage of its GDP, for instance in the period from 1987-96 it spent an average of 7.5% of its GDP. In contrast India spent an average of 2.8% of its GDP from the 1987-96

---

[46] JDW, India Budget May Affect Modernisation, 1998, Pg29

[47] JDW, India's Search for a New SPG, 1994, Pg45

[48] Flight International, Airforces of the World Directory, Marketforce Ltd, 1998, Pg68

[49] JDW, Indian Budget Fall May Affect Modernisation, 1998, Pg29

[50] Stockholm International Peace Research Institute (SIPRI), World Military Expenditure Prices 1987-96, Oxford University Press, 1997, Pg197

[51] India to spend $200 bn on defence systems by 2022 - https://www.hindustantimes.com/delhi-news/india-to-spend-200-bn-on-defence-systems-by-2022/story-K2MzbLCRGranHRyrsii5SJ.html

period. However this is because the Indian economy is growing at a better rate than Pakistan.[53]

According to Stockholm International Peace Research Institute (SIPRI) in 2015 - India spent around 2.3 % of its GDP on military, which was $51.3 billion and Pakistan spent 3.4% of their GDP on military, which is $9.5 billion.[54]

Year (SIPRI)	India		Pakistan	
	GDP	Amount in USD	GDP	Amount in USD
2005	2.8%	35,718	3.7%	7,032
2006	2.5%	36,151	3.4%	7,081
2007	2.3%	41,003	3.1%	6,676
2008	2.6%	48,277	3.1%	6,879
2009	2.9%	48,470	3.1%	7,134
2010	2.7%	48,940	3.1%	7,520
2011	2.6%	48,766	3.3%	7,975
2012	2.5%	48,406	3.2%	8,238
2013	2.4%	50,914	3.3%	8,655
2014	2.5%	51,116	3.3%	9,248
2015	2.3%	51,257	3.4%	9,510

Data source SIPRI

Pakistan spends a high proportion of its GDP on military expenditure, to balance Indian military superiority. However, in real terms India spends on average nearly three times more on military expenditure than Pakistan does. For example, in 1998, Indian expenditure was $9.9bn compared to Pakistan's $3.2bn.[55] This equates to just over three times more than Pakistan spends, thereby encouraging Pakistan to spend a higher proportion of its GDP to try to minimally match India's military capabilities. India spent nearly four times more on military expenditure in 2017. India had become largest arms importer from 1950-2017, importing a massive $119.89 billion worth of weapons.

---

[52] International Institute for Strategic Studies (IISS), Military Balance 1998-99, Oxford University Press, 1998, Pg155-160

[53] SIPRI 1997, op cit:203

[54] Freya Dasgupta (2016) Who Spends More On Their Military, India Or Pakistan? - https://www.outlookindia.com/blog/story/who-spends-more-on-their-military-india-or-pakistan/3837

[55] IISS, op cit:155-160

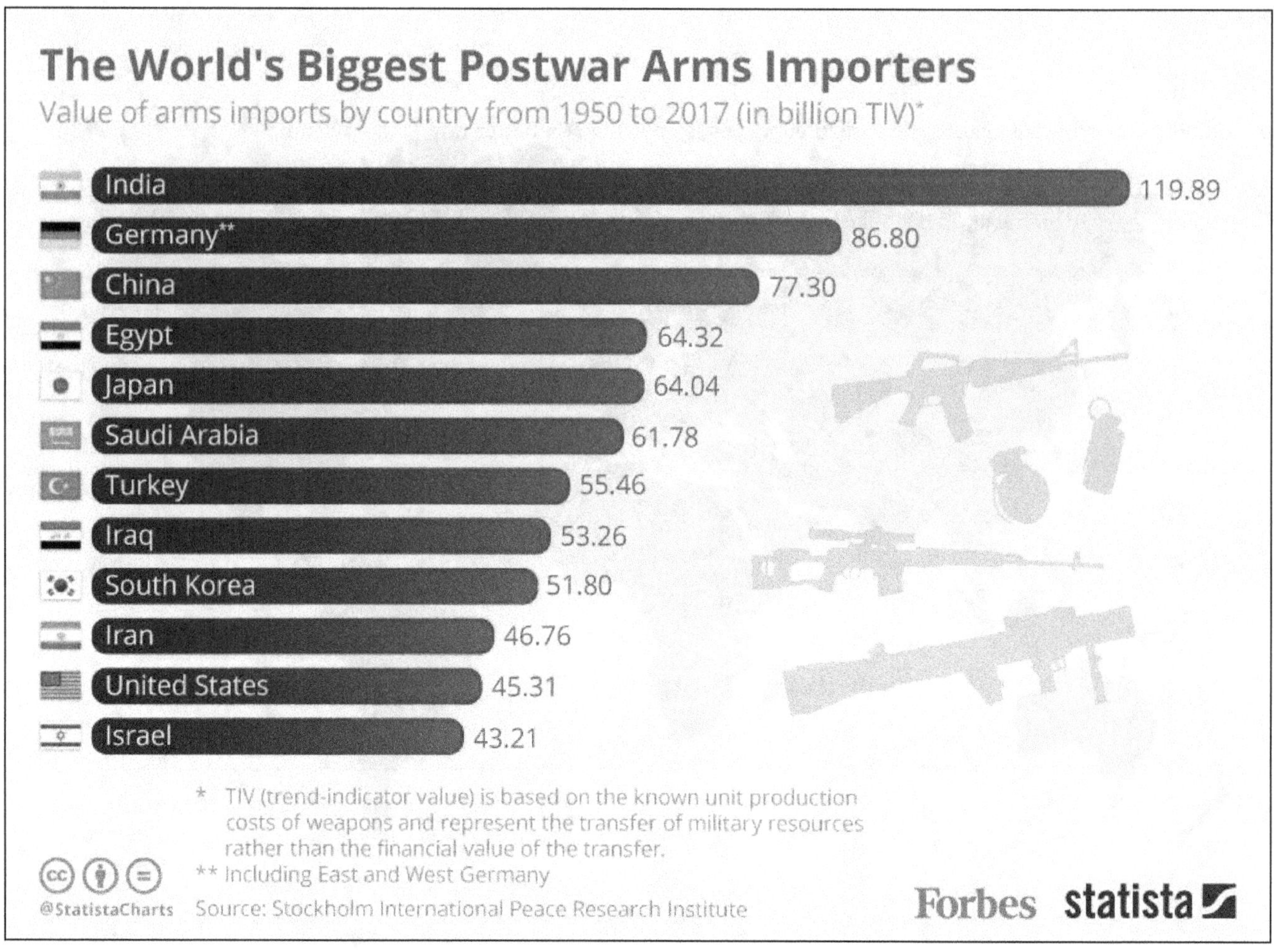

The World's Biggest Arms Importers Since 1950[56]

India's military superiority over Pakistan becomes even clearer as one examines the details of the military balance.

The Balance of Land Forces

According to the International Institute for Strategic Studies (The Military Balance 2018), quantitative differences in the number of men and weapons gave the following ratios between India and Pakistan. India enjoys an over two-to-one advantage in army personnel (1,200,000 to 560,000).[57] The superiority further increases to approximately 5.6 to 1 if paramilitary personnel are taken into account (over 1,585,950 million to almost 282,000). India's superiority in army manpower is matched by its overall advantage over Pakistan in nearly all categories of ground combat equipment. In main battle tanks (MBT), the Indian advantage is approximately 1.5 to one (4,197 to 2,737), in mechanised infantry vehicles (APCs/AIFV/Recce) approximately 1.7 to one (2,836 to 1,715), in artillery 2.2 to one (9,684 to 4,472), and in multi-role helicopters 3.6 to one (787 to 216). In only one area, attack helicopters, does Pakistan enjoy an advantage which is 2.2 to one (42 to 19).[58]

The ratios cited above are based on the total number of each type of equipment in the respective inventories. They do not take into account the qualitative differences of their ground force equipment. Thus, in addition to its obvious quantitative advantage, India also enjoys a qualitative advantage in most categories of equipment as well.

---

[56] The World's Biggest Arms Importers Since 1950 - https://www.forbes.com/sites/niallmccarthy/2018/03/12/the-worlds-biggest-post-war-arms-importers-infographic/#32e3fa118e34

[57] Ibid
[58] Ibid

Indian 'Nag' anti-tank missile

All in all, India maintains a large army consisting of well over 1.2 million men, supported by a large reserve force consisting of 960,000 men. The standing army is distributed into three armoured divisions, six semi-armoured divisions (RAPID), 35 infantry and mountain divisions, fifteen independent brigades.[59] Pakistan sees this large military build-up as Pakistan-specific. They argue that the mechanised and armoured forces, with a total of 4,197 tanks, cannot be used against the island of Sri Lanka, nor in the soggy terrain of Bangladesh. They are also not needed in the mountains of tiny Nepal and cannot cross the mighty Himalayan mountain ranges towards China, Pakistan, clearly, is the target.[60]

IAF Su-30 MKI Flanker fighter aircraft on a training exercise with US F-15 Eagle combat aircraft.

---

[59] Ibid
[60] The News International, Armed to the Teeth, Jang Publishers Ltd, 1998, Pg10

Pakistan's Shaheen 3 Nuclear capable ballistic missile

<u>The Balance of Air Forces</u>

The recent Gulf War and also the war in Kosova (NATO's air war) has shown that the outcome of any future conflict will rest heavily on control of the skies and the ability to deny the enemy of the same. The Indian Air Force (IAF) is the 4th largest in the world and growing rapidly. It justifies its size by pointing to the Chinese PLAAF (Peoples Liberation Army Air Force).[61]

In comparison to Pakistan Air force, Indian again enjoys a sizeable advantage in this field too. In personnel strength, it has almost a 1.8 to 1 advantage (127,200 to 70,000). In terms of operational units, the Indian Air Force (IAF) has a 3.6 to one edge in ground attack fighter squadrons (29 to 8), two to one in air-defence fighter squadrons this time in Pakistan's adavantage (6 to 3), and two to one in reconnaissance squadrons (2 to 1). In terms of equipment, the IAF has a better than 2 to 1 advantage in jet combat aircraft (849 to 425) and over 6.9 to one in transports (241 to 35).[62]

An important area for comparison is the number of sophisticated fighter in each air force. For the Pakistan Air force (PAF), its most capable aircraft include the F-16 (76), the JF-17 Thunder (85), the Mirage 3 (82) and the Mirage 5 (89) of which there are a total of 332. In comparison, the IAF has a better than 1.6 to one advantage with total of 546 aircraft that could be considered state-of-the-art including Mirage 2000s (50), Jaguars (117), Mig-27s (65), Mig-29s (62), LCA Tejas (2), and the SU-30MK (250).[63]

---

[61] JDW, Country Survey-India, 1990, Pg1023
[62] IISS, op cit:155-160
[63] Ibid

IAF Jaguar attack aircraft

While the IAF has a numerical advantage, it also has a qualitative advantage over the Pakistan Air force, which it will retain under any currently foreseeable conditions. Qualitatively, the IAF must also be considered one of the best-equipped services in the World. The majority of India's combat aircraft are comparable to front-line NATO/WTP aircraft. It is also virtually certain that the Indian advantage in the air will continue to contribute far more support of the Indian Army than the PAF can contribute to the support of the Pakistan Army.[64]

It is also important to note that the F-16A/Cs and other aircraft in the PAF will not face a Mig-21 or Mig-23 threat in the late 2018s. They will face an Indian threat equipped with the state-of-the-art Russian fighters like the SU-30MKI and the MIG 29, French fighters like the Mirage 2000, and a wide range of new Western/Russian systems in Indian forces.[65] The Indian Air Force has also ordered the sophisticated French Rafael multi-role combat aircraft – these aircrafts would poise extra threats to the PAF.

All in all, among its ranks the IAF contains Mirage 2000H aircraft, Mig-27 attack aircraft, Mig-29 interceptors and Anglo-French Jaguar deep-strike attack aircraft. The bombers and a large transport fleet is in addition. For their protection there are 30 surface-to-air missile squadrons. Also existing fleets of 125 Mig-21 bis and 65 Mig-27s are being updated. The development of India's Light Combat Aircraft (LCA) has been completed and orders have been made – the IAF plans to induct up to 324 LCA Tejas[66] multi-role combat aircraft.[67]

---

[64] Cordesman, op cit:132

[65] Cordesman, op cit:182

[66] IAF commits to 324 Tejas fighters, provided a good Mark-II jet is delivered - https://timesofindia.indiatimes.com/india/iaf-commits-to-324-tejas-fighters-provided-a-good-mark-2-jet-is-delivered/articleshow/63306776.cms

[67] Flight International, op cit:68

Over and above this, India has purchased 250 modern Russian built state of the art SU-30MK force-multiplier multi-role fighter aircraft. Especially with the recent acquisition of the SU-30MKIs, the IAF has at least on paper, tremendously improved its qualitative standing. With the force listed above, the IAF is capable of using the latest 'smart' weaponry, stand-off weapons, extremely long range air-to-air missiles such as the AA-10 Alamo and countless other lethal stores. It is also capable of delivering nuclear weapons deep inside Pakistani territory.[68]

IAF sophisticated Russian Made Su-30MKI Flanker multi-role combat aircraft

India is also steadily improving the quality of its air weaponry and is obtaining some of the latest and most capable Russian air-to-air and air-to-ground munitions. Qualitative enhancements in IAF aircraft include 'BVR' or Beyond Visual Range capability. This allows a fighter pilot to track, lock and destroy a target while it is far away. The IAF has recently acquired AA-10 Alamo missiles which will allow such attacks to be made against Pakistani aircraft at a range of more than 100km. This greatly reduces the chances of aerial combat coming down to dogfights, where pilot's skill is the deciding factor and an area in which the Pakistan Air Force has the qualitative edge. All SU-30MKIs and Mig-29s have BVR capability whereas the PAF had limited capability. In addition, the longest-range air-to-air missiles in the Pakistan Air Force is the AIM-7 Sparrow which has barely 1/3rd the range of an Alamo.[69] For the PAF things had gradually improved when a large amount of US Amraam BVR missiles were ordered, In addition the Chinese SD-10 BVR missile has been ordered for its JF-17 Thunder multi-role combat aircraft. This gives the PAF the same advantage as the IAF have had with their BVR missiles.

Furthermore, the IAF has also taken due note of the electronic spectrum which had successfully paralysed Iraqi air defences and command communications during the Gulf War. India has developed the capability to use EW technology to cripple command and communications of adversary's Army, Navy and Air Force. IAF has acquired a wide range of BVR munitions. Such capabilities have greatly enhanced the offensive and defensive capabilities of the IAF.[70]

---

[68] Brassey's, World Aircraft & Systems Directory, Brassey's Ltd, 1996, Pg92
[69] India Today, Future Fire, 1998, Pg22
[70] Ibid

PAF US made F-16 Falcon combat aircraft - its most sophisticated type in its inventory

In contrast to the IAF, the Pakistan Air force (PAF) is much smaller, and is also far less modern. The PAF's 425 combat aircraft now include only 76 sophisticated F-16s and 85 JF-17 Thunder combat aircrafts. Its only other comparatively modern fighters are 171 last-generation Mirage 3/5s. The majority of the PAF consists of Chinese combat aircraft such as the F-7P/PG interceptors; these are Chinese variants of the old Russian Mig-21 (mid-aircraft 1960s vintage). It has also purchased updated Chinese F-7M (MIG-21) fighters. These aircrafts are capable of combat close to Pakistan's borders, but lack the capability to strike deep into Indian territory.[71]

PAF F-7P Interceptors

In view of the limited strategic depth of the country, Pakistani air bases are located within striking range of Indian aircraft. If they choose, the Indians can base their aircraft deep into their own territory, but still have the range to reach the border area where the battle will likely occur. The PAF badly needs to replace its F-7P/PG and some of its older Mirage combat aircraft, most of which are obsolete or obsolescent and lack modern avionics, weaponry and performance capability. It is trying to solve this problem by the purchase and modification of large numbers of its co-developed Chinese and Pakistani fighter – the JF-17 Thunder multi-role combat

---

[71] Cordesman, op cit:133

aircraft.[72] It is thought that the PAF could be ordering between 250–300 JF-17 Thunder aircraft in total, which would give a significant boost to the PAF in inducting modern sophisticated aircraft.

PAF JF-17 combat aircrat armed with BVR missile

Overall, since 1989, the PAF has shrunk due to the non-procurement of aircraft and weapons, and the air power imbalance, if allowed to continue, will threaten its national security beyond repair. The American Pressler Amendment has denied the duly paid-for F-16 fighters (71 had been ordered) and access to other US-made fighter, radars or missiles.[73] Furthermore, Pakistan's Chief of the Air Staff recently stated that, Air power will be decisive factor in any future conflict. Future wars will start with air power, and defeat and victory will be decided when either side concedes defeat in the air.[74]

<u>The Balance of Naval Forces</u>

As is the case with air and ground forces, India's Navy enjoys numeric as well as qualitative superiority over Pakistan. India has conducted large-scale modernisation and expansion programmes to improve its ability to exercise sea control and denial and to ensure security of its coastline and island territories against any major naval power. In the 1971 Indo-Pakistani war, the Indian Navy was able to carry out a successful sea blockade of Pakistan's only major port.[75]

---

[72] Ibid
[73] JDW, A Loss of Momentum, 1997, Pg45
[74] Ibid
[75] Cordesman, op cit:182

Indian Navy aircraft carrier launching its Mig-29 combat aircraft for a sortie

Today, India has a large Navy, which continues to grow. At present, it has one aircraft carriers, 14 submarines, 14 missile destroyers, 13 frigates, 108 missile boats and corvettes, supported by fighter and long range reconnaissance aircraft and 83 armed helicopters. It has over a 17 landing craft with an amphibious list capability of 1,200 strong marine force with their arms and equipment. This large force poses a potent threat to Pakistan and the other nearby states of the Indian Ocean.[76]

IN aircraft carrier – giving India the ability to strike at long rages (Power proection capability)

---

[76] IISS, op cit:155-160

Indian Navy carrier battle group

In contrast, Pakistan has no aircraft carriers, it only has 8 submarines, 0 missiles destroyers, 10 frigates, 17 missile boats and corvettes, supported by 7 medium range maritime patrol aircraft and 12 armed helicopters. It has 1,200 strong marine force with their arms and equipment. This small force does not pose a potent threat to India.

In terms of personnel, the Indian advantage is approximately 2.5 to one (58,350 to 23,800). In major surface combatants, India enjoys a better than 2.8 to one advantage (28 to 10). Of particular note is the fact that India has one aircraft carrier, whereas Pakistan has none. The Indian Navy also enjoys a 1.8 to one advantage in submarines (14 to 8) and a better than 6.9 to one edge in maritime patrol aircraft (48 to 7).[77]

IN Submarine

---

[77] Ibid

IN carrier battle group

On the whole, the Indian Navy is a formidable force when compared with other navies in the area. No local navy, including the Pakistani Navy, is able to compete on the open seas with the Indian Navy. Pakistan's naval units (surface, combatants, submarines, naval aircraft), cannot prevent India from attacking Pakistan's coastline. Only the acquisition of the AM-39 Exocet air-to-surface missile (ASM) for the Naval Air Arm, and the Harpoon surface-to-surface missile (SSM) for surface combatants, gives Pakistan even a limited capability to inflict losses on Indian vessels operating in its territorial waters.

All in all, the Pakistani Navy is a small force capable of defending its own coastal waters. In combination with 'Exocet' armed- Mirages, the Pakistani Navy (PN) might be able to keep the Indian Navy away from the port of Karachi, and could make an amphibious operation costly, but it is no match for the Indian Navy away from the Pakistani coast.[78] Pakistan has also ordered new sophisticated long range anti-ship missiles from China and has currently tested its own missiles – these should give the PN the ability to inflict serious losses to a hostile power.

---

[78] Cordesman, op cit:182

PAF JF-17 Thunder multi-role combat aircraft demonstartings its anti-ship capabilities

PN warships

PN tests its US made Harpoon anti-ship missile

Pakistan Navy's Zarb ASCM is seen here being test-launched from a TEL vehicle during exercise 'Sealion III'.

The following table will show the military imbalance between India and Pakistan.

Pakistan-India Conventional Military Balance 2018

Conventional Military Balance	India	Pakistan
Defence Budgets	Rs3.60tr ($52.5bn)	Rs1.02tr ($9.72bn)
Army **(Total Military Personnel)**	1,200,000 (Active) Reserves 960,000 **Paramilitary forces** 1,585,950 active	560,000 (Active) Reserves 500,000 **Paramilitary forces** 282,000 active
Tanks	4197+ 1,025+ **T-90s** 1,950 **T-72M1 Ajeya**, 122 **Arjun MK.1** (1,100 **various models in store**)	2737+ 21 **Al-Khalid I** 300 **Al-Khalid** (MBT 2000) 320 **T-80UD**, 275+ **T- 85II AP**, 51 **T-54/T-55**, 400 **T-69**, 1,100 **T-59/Al-Zarrar** (270 **M-48A5** in store)
APCs	2,836 (Including **AIFV/ RECCE**)	1,715 **M**-113
Artillery	9,684+ (Including self-propelled artillery)	4,472 (Including self-propelled artillery)

		38 **AH-1F/S Cobra** (Army)
Helicopters (Combat)	19 **Mi-25/Mi35 Hind** (Air Force)	4 **Mi-35M Hind**
<u>**Air Force (Active personnel)**</u>	140,000 (Reserves 140,000)	70,000 (Reserves 8,000)
Combat Aircraft	849 combat capable	425 combat capable
	250 **Su-30MKI-II** 62 **MIG-29/UB**, 50 **Mirage** 2000H/TH, 117 **Jaguar IS/IT/IM**, 65 **MIG-27ML**, 20 **MIG-23 UB**, 174 **MIG-21BIS** (for **MIG-21-**93 upgrade) **MIG-21 U/FL/U**, 2 **LCA/Tejas** (+**109** Various – not indicated in military balance2018)	76 **F-16 A/B/C/D**, 93 **F-7P/PG/FT-7 Airguard/Skybolt** (**MIG-21**), 85 **JF-17 Thunder**, 82 **Mirage III B/EP**,OD/R 51(+38) **Mirage V PA/DPA,PA-2/DPA-3** (38 not indicated in military balance 2018, assumed to be Mirage 5)
<u>**Navy (Active personnel)**</u>	58,350 (Reserves 55,000)	23,800 (Reserves 5,000)
	Aircraft Carriers 1 **Submarines** 14 **Destroyers** 14 **Frigates** 13 **Patrol and Coastal**	**Aircraft Carriers** None **Submarines** 8 **Destroyers** 0 **Frigates** 10 **Patrol and Coastal**

Combatants	Combatants	17
(Corvettes/Missile Craft) 108	(Corvettes/Missile Craft)	

Source: The IISS Military Balance 2018,[79]

The Overall Military Imbalance

American intelligence experts privately estimate that the Pakistan Armed Forces could defeat against an Indian invasion for only a few days to a few weeks. This accurately reflects the numerical imbalance in each side's force strength and order of battle. Pakistan will do better on the defensive than in the attack. India has superior static defence capabilities and the mass to counterattack quickly and effectively. Pakistan forces, however, are better structured for a manoeuvre style of warfare and could inflict serious losses on any invading force. And keeping in view the above mentioned Indian superiority in conventional arms, Pakistan then chose to take shelter under the nuclear umbrella.[80]

Pakistan's sees only one major motive for building this large military establishment, which it perceives far beyond its legitimate defence and security requirements can only be found in India's desire for regional hegemony.[81] Indian perceptions of threat to her sovereignty from her small neighbours emerge from its own past and present policies of attempting to subdue the whole of South Asia to her will.

IN firepower

---

[79] IISS, Chapter 6 Asia
[80] Cordesman, op cit:131
[81] Malik, op cit:152

Pakistan Army Personnel along with mechanized troops in the training exercise 'Al Buraq II' held at Kotri Field Firing Ranges.

Strategy – India and Pakistan

In order to achieve success in a military conflict, then it is essential that strategy and tactics employed are valid. Strategy is seen as the planning, organising, coordinating, managing, and general direction of military operations to meet overall political and military goals. The strategy is implemented by the tactics chosen in battlefield - Carl Von Clausewitz, the great military theorist said "Tactics is the art of using troops in battle; strategy is the art of using battles to win the war."[82] Strategy and tactics have changed over time, primarily due to the new technology available and hence have been viewed differently. It is viewed that in some circumstances it has become difficult to distinguish tactics from strategy as both are interdependent on each other. Strategy is restricted by what tactics are plausible; particularly the size, training, and morale of forces, type and number of weapons available, terrain, weather, and quality and location of enemy forces, the tactics to be used are reliant on strategic concerns.

The strategies employed by both India and Pakistan have all began to evolve over the last few decades. They have changed due to the technological requirements and the adversaries capabilities. We will look at the following strategies in detail, **India's Cold Start doctrine (CSD)** and **Pakistan's New Concept of War Fighting (NCWF):**

India – Cold Start Military doctrine

---

[82] Strategy and Tactics - http://www.molossia.org/milacademy/strategy.html

Cold Start is an evolving doctrine undertaken by the Indian Armed Forces as a counter-measure to the Pakistani Armed Forces under the shadow of two declared nuclear powers. Under the nuclear umbrella, war becomes dangerously a non-option as any misadventure moves could escalate tensions to a nuclear exchange. The potential nuclear exchange would devastate the South Asian region as well effect the global environment.

Indian army chief General Bipin Rawat

The Indian Armed Forces have devised the 'cold start' doctrine as a way initiating a limited rapid conflict and believes that the limited attack on Pakistan would not force Pakistan to use its nuclear weapons. The Indian Armed Forces had denied that any such doctrine existed and it was only when the Indian army chief, Bipin Rawat confirmed its existence in an interview.[83]

Cold Start in essence is a limited war strategy that envisages of seizing Pakistani territory on a rapid basis without resorting to any nuclear exchange. The strategy believes that it can take Pakistani territory before it crosses the Pakistani 'red lines' and hence believe that Pakistan would not resort to a nuclear strike – which could result in a full scale nuclear war. The doctrine has its root from the terrorist attacks on the Indian Parliament in 2001 and was thought to have been masterminded in Pakistan (which has robustly denied any form of involvement). Any terrorist attack in India that is assumed to come from Pakistan would trigger India to put into action its Cold Start doctrine.

Indian exercise to ensure that India is fully capable of implementing Cold Start doctrine

The resulting terrorist attack on its parliament and the slow mobilisation of its Strike Corps to the borders with Pakistan resulted in Pakistan rapidly strengthening its defensive positions and thereby nullifying any impending attach

---

[83] https://www.economist.com/blogs/economist-explains/2017/02/economist-explains

from India (by increasing the costs of an incursion and whether it can succeed in its objectives). Cold Start is a strategy to improve this in the future – by essentially having a well organised and special integrated units that are stationed closer to the border would enable India to inflict serious harm before any international pressure to stop hostilities and by pursuing its limited aims, it is assumed that this will deny Pakistan a justification of launching a nuclear strike.

In contrast to the Cold Start doctrine, Pakistan's Prime Minister Shahid Khaqan Abbasi has confirmed that the short range nuclear missile has been developed to counter India's flawed cold start strategy.[84] The Basic evolution of the Cold Start doctrine, is as follows:

1. The terrorist incident on 13 December 2001 was blamed on Pakistan and led to widespread pressures on the Indian Government to take punitive action on its neighbour.

2. Operation Parakram was initiated and Indian troops were mobilised to take action against Pakistan. However, by the time the Indian army's three mechanised strike corps were mobilised to the border and were ready to launch their tanks and infantry combat vehicles (all tools at its disposal), Pakistan's defensive formations were deployed and ready to counter-attack and beat the Indian strike formations with its own strike divisions.[85]

3. It took three weeks for India's Three Strike corps to mobilise and take up positions on the border with Pakistan. This allowed Pakistan to further strengthen its defensive positions and reduced the element of surprise and ensured that the Indian attack would become costly (and could lead to a nuclear strike).

4. Furthermore, this delay in mobilising enabled other international players, such as the US to pressurise India to stop any planned hostilities against Pakistan. The US and its allies had their own interest and were on an offensive against Taliban forces in Afghanistan and did not want Pakistan to stop this as it would affect the logistics of operations in Afghanistan.

5. The slow mobilisation from the Indian Strike Corps led to the development of the Cold Start doctrine. This doctrine plans to attack Pakistan (by rapidly mobilising infantry and armour to launch lightning strikes across the border) within 48 hours of any major provocation or terror attack (that is linked to Pakistan). The plan is to strike and penetrate into Pakistan before its defensive formations can prepare and occupy defensive positions along the border without escalating into a nuclear war.

6. Cold Start is based on two key goals. The first is to readjust its 'Pivot' corps (defensive or ground holding corps) so that it can launch an offensive operation virtually from a 'cold start' and deny Pakistan the advantage of early mobilisation. The second goal was to ensure that India had a number of integrated divisional-size forces launching operations to capture Pakistani territory along the international boundary. The plan is for the integrated battle groups (IBGs) to allow India's strike corps to take advantages of any success achieved. Any captured Pakistani territory would be used as a bargaining tools to stop any alleged proxy war support. These IBGs are to be fully integrated with the Indian Air Force, Naval aviation and to be able to launch multiple strikes round the clock into Pakistan. It is thought that each IBG will be the size of a division (30,000-50,000 troops) and highly mobile unlike the main strike corps.

7. The Indian Military believes that the cold start doctrine would deter Pakistan from waging any proxy war or major provocation by sending a clear message of Indian capability to attack. However, Pakistan sees this as a dangerous

---

[84] http://www.livemint.com/Politics/hpSChKODtfe7Pba34i2rOJ/Cold-Start-doctrine-A-10point-guide-to-Indias-military-st.html

[85] https://thewire.in/101586/cold-start-pakistan-doctrine/

doctrine that is inherently escalatory, by forcing the Pakistani armed forces into relocating defensive formations close to the Indian border. In addition, it has compelled the Pakistan army to develop its 'Nasr' (Hatf-IX victory) short-range nuclear missile (small yield nuclear bomb), this is a highly destabilising "tactical nuclear weapons" (TNWs) – to halt an Indian Cold Start strike.

The Indian army has inducted the Russian BM-30 Smerch 300MM multiple-launch rocket systems (MLRS). The Smerch has 300mm rockets with a firing range of 70 - 90 km and able to fire a salvo of 12 rockets in 38 seconds) and could neutralise a large target area.

Indian MBT on exercise to validate Cold Start Doctrine.

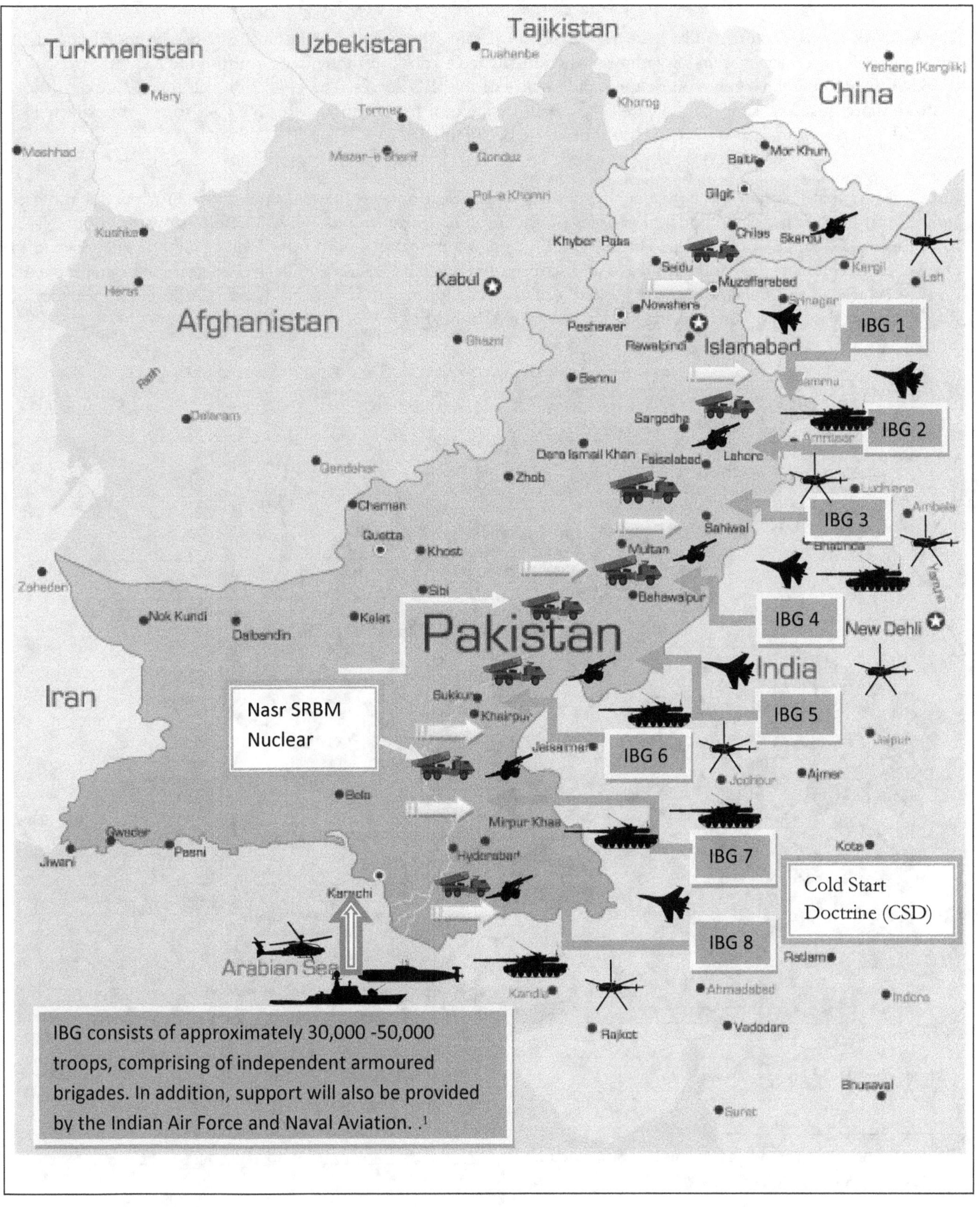

Turkmenistan
Uzbekistan
Tajikistan
Dushanbe
China
Yecheng (Kargilik)
Mary
Termez
Khorog
Mashhad
Mazar-e Sharif
Qonduz
Batu
Mor Khun
Pol-e Khomri
Gilgit
Kushka
Chilas
Skardu
Khyber Pass
Kargil
Herat
Seidu
Muzaffarabad
Leh
Afghanistan
Kabul
Srinagar
Nowshera
IBG 1
Ghazni
Peshawar
Rawalpindi
Islamabad
Jammu
Bannu
Sargodha
Amritsar
IBG 2
Dera Ismail Khan
Faisalabad
Lahore
Ludhiana
Zhob
Ambala
Qandahar
Sahiwal
IBG 3
Bhatinda
Chaman
Multan
Quetta
Khost
Bahawalpur
IBG 4
New Dehli
Zahedan
Sibi
Pakistan
India
Nok Kundi
Kalat
Dalbandin
Iran
Sukkur
IBG 5
Nasr SRBM
Nuclear
Khairpur
Jaisalmer
IBG 6
Jaipur
Jodhpur
Ajmer
Bela
Kota
Gwadar
Mirpur Khas
Jiwani
Pasni
Hyderabad
IBG 7
Cold Start
Doctrine (CSD)
Karachi
IBG 8
Ratlam
Arabian Sea
Kandla
Ahmadabad
Indore
Rajkot
Vadodara
Bhusaval
Surat
IBG consists of approximately 30,000 -50,000
troops, comprising of independent armoured
brigades. In addition, support will also be provided
by the Indian Air Force and Naval Aviation. .[1]

The Cold Start doctrine aims to deny Pakistan justification to resort to its nuclear first-use option by inflicting rapid, fatal and limited attacks.[86] The air force and naval aviation would accompany the land forces in the single or multiples strikes in a limited area till the objectives are achieved "within hours". [87]

Through Cold Start doctrine, India believes that it can paralyse or reduce a Pakistani response by mobilising eight IBGs to enter its territory within 72-96 hours when instructed to do. India intends to confuse the Pakistani troops by breaking their formational cohesion by the rapid attckes of the IBG forces. The confusion will force Pakistan troops to make more mistakes, similar to the 1940s German blitkrieg of its neighbours. India's IBG forces are expected to make 50-80 km teritorial gains once the hostilities have been inititated.

India believes that Pakistan will not launch its short-range nuclear missiles (Nasr) at the outset of hostilities and presume that if they do use tactical nuclear missiles on the invading Indian troops – it will be on its own territory. Naser has an estimated range of 60-70 km. This is agin a folly and a miscalculation on the Indian side – hostilities tend to change the direction of the conflict. India in all its frustration has not been able to decively defeat Pakistan, despite its massive economic and military strength – it had only suceeded in the 1971 War, with Pakistan losing its territory of East Pakistan (Bangladesh) due to a big foreign sponsored insurgency.

Pakistan's battlefield nuclear capable Nasr missile

---

[86] Naveed Ahmed (2017) India's Elusive Cold Start doctrine - https://tribune.com.pk/story/1300686/indias-elusive-cold-start-doctrine-pakistans-military-preparedness/

[87] Masood Ur Rehman Khattak – Indian Military's Cold Start Doctrine RP-32-Masood-Indian-Militarys-Cold-Start-Doctrine-Mar-2011.pdf

Pakistan armed forces have taken a number of measures to deal with India's desire for regional hegemonistic tendencies, where it can brow beat its neighbours. It too has evolved its own strategies to deal with the threat to its territorial integrity and its dispute over Kashmir. India's leaders are continuing their hostile behavious against their neighbour – with the Hindu fundamentalist government of the BJP, Prime minister Narendra Modi has continued with the hostile posturing at a different levels, in the same way as the former BJP prime minister Atal Bihari Vajpayee had done when it conducted its second nuclear test in Pokran. Since Vajpayee tested nuclear weapons in 1998, Pakistan does not believe in India's stance of no-first use. This is more paramount in the current era in which Pakistan is prepared for India opting to nuclear first-use - especially with the current hawkish hindu fundamentalists like Manohar Parrikar, Ajit Davol and Sushma Sawraj at the helm of the BJP government.[88]

For Pakistan, its battle hardened armed forces have adapted to undertake any future hostilities from India or other external threats. The 17 years of conflict in Afghanistan and its spill effect on Pakistan territory via numerous terrorism has enable Pakistan to successfully deal with this threat.

Pakistan has significantly upgraded its defence preparedness and refinement of its military doctrine. It has increased joint operations training amongst all it services. It's refined New Concept of Warfare has been developed to deal with all forms of threats, especially its Cold Start doctrine.

A100 multiple-launch rocket systems (MLRS) of the Pakistani Army

---

[88] https://tribune.com.pk/story/1300686/indias-elusive-cold-start-doctrine-pakistans-military-preparedness

Key Elements in the Indian Cold Start doctrine (CSD)

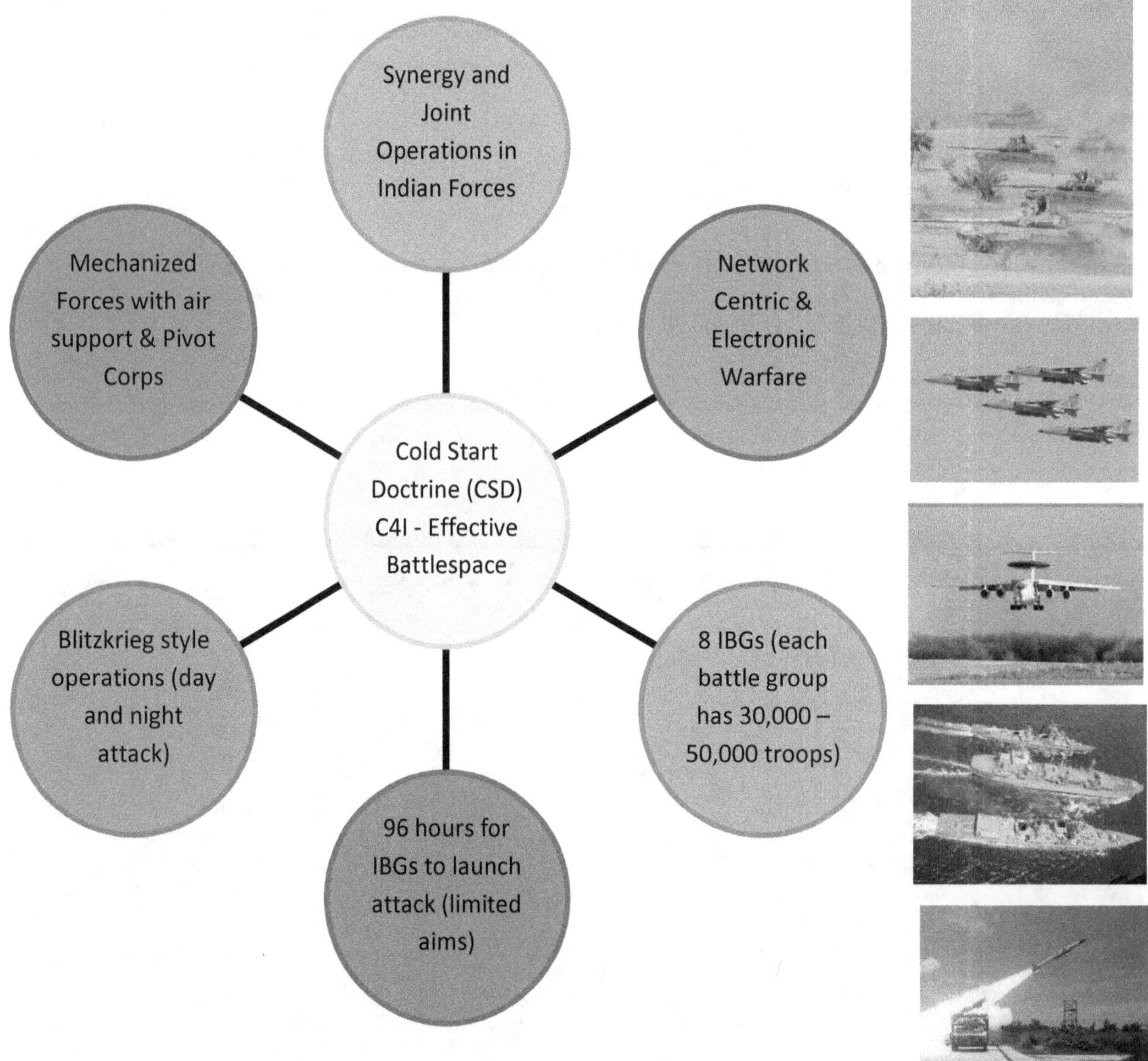

Effective battlespace is term used to signify a unified and integrated military strategy to achieve an overall mission objectives in combined operations. A combination , information, air, land, sea, cyber warfare, space and evolving technologies to achieve military goals. In order to apply effective combat power, other factors such as the environment/terrain, hostile and friendly forces disposition, weather and the area of the influence. In addition, a a robust Command, Control, Communications, Computers, and Intelligence (C4I) needs to be integrated to ensure a decisive edge is maintained of the battlespace."[89]

---

[89] http://www.c4i.org/whatisc4i.html

Pakistan's New Concept of War Fighting (NCWF):

In order to counter India's Cold Start doctrine (CSD), Pakistan has refined its own strategy and this has now evolved into a New Concept of War Fighting (NCWF) doctrine. This Pakistani doctrine is seen as a major counter balance to India's CSD.[90]

Pakistan military exercises, Azm-e-Nau.

The Azm-e-Nau (New Resolve) Games took place from 2009 -2013 and were essentially exercises to validate Pakistan's new doctrine (NCWF). The war games were the largest ever conducted by the Pakistan armed forces since the Zarb-e-Momin exercises held in 1989 — which had validated its 'offensive defence' doctrine at the time.[91]

---

[90] Pakistan develops new war doctrine to counter India -
https://www.indiatoday.in/world/story/pakistan-develops-new-war-doctrine-to-counter-india-166997-2013-06-17

[91] Azm-e-Nau 3: Largest Military Exercise by Pakistan Army - http://www.chowrangi.pk/azm-e-nau-3-largest-military-exercise-by-pakistan-army.html

According to the Inter-Services Public Relations (ISPR), the war games were meant to operationalize new strategies against evolving threats in the country. The conclusion of the 4 years of war gaming and exercises resulted in Pakistani military adopting the new NCWF doctrine, primarily aimed ad pre-empting/disrupting Indians CSD.[92]

The exercises had involved between 30,000- 50,000 troops with the usage of various aircraft and equipment of the Pakistan Air Force. The exercises were conducted whilst 150,000 troops were still engaged in the fight with the Taliban (TTP) on its western border. This new resolve indicated to Pakistan's adversaries that it is able to defend any part of its territory – whether western or eastern border.

The key areas of the NCWF are as follows:

- Improve mobilisation
- Joint coordination of the Army, Air Force and Navy response to any conventional threat.

According to Brigadier Dr Muhammad Khan, Azm-e-Nau puts a checkmate to India's CSD.[93] The war games/exercises were conducted in different phases to test and evaluate different mission scenarios.

Phase-I	In this phase, various scenarios were given and executed and appropriate military plans were refined after evaluation of the exercises (at this stage, it was primarily indoor war games, consisting of substantial map exercises. In addition, numerous operational constraints were injected in to the scenarios and further evaluations were made at the execution of the plans.
Phase-II	The operational plans from phase 1 were executed through physical trials in the field exercises. Any hurdles or shortcomings were further refined after putting the troops through the exercises. The Pakistan Air Force (PAF) and the Pakistan Navy (PN) also participated in these exercises.
Phase-III	Further refinements are made – troops are split in to two groups, Blue Land (defendant) and Fox land (enemy) are put to their paces in the battleground. Mechanised forces (Tanks/armoured personnel carriers), with combination of support provided by the PAF and PN. Conventional firepower of all types has been demonstrated, enhanced training in intelligence gathering, surveillance, reconnaissance and communication means have been checked (network centric warfare capabilities).
Phase IV	The final phase of the war games were undertaken during June 2013. The PAF and the PN have jointly worked with the Army and increased the synergy and integration amongst the services. This was shown by the impressive demonstrations of the armoured, artillery, air defence, army aviation formations and firepower by the PAFs F-16, JF-17 Thunder, F-7P and Mirage fighter aircraft (repelling attacks by enemy forces). The war games were carried out with different formations and at different levels – this was to increase combat readiness, and to identify problems in logistics, training, and to validate its new military doctrine (NCWF).

These exercises had evolved into making the New Concept of War Fighting (NCWF) an updated doctrine for the Pakistan Armed Forces – it is believed to have countered India's Cold start doctrine (CSD) effectively.

---

[92] Pakistan develops new war doctrine to counter India -
https://www.indiatoday.in/world/story/pakistan-develops-new-war-doctrine-to-counter-india-166997-2013-06-17

[93] Brig Dr Muhammad Khan - http://hilal.gov.pk/index.php/component/k2/item/642-from-cold-start-to-cold-storage

New concept seeks to improve troop mobilization time and to increase joint operations within the three services (Army, Navy and Air Force synergy).

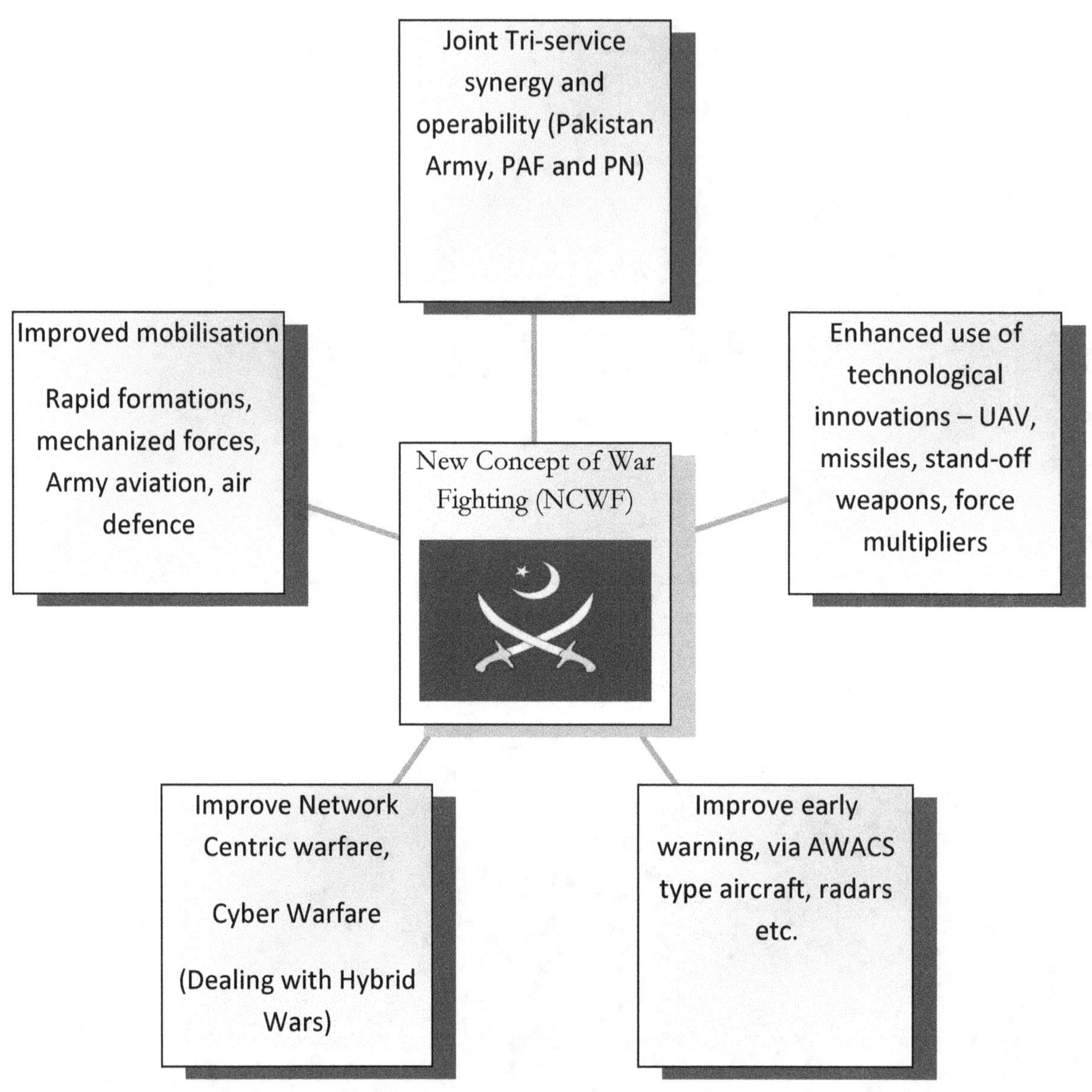

In essence the Pakistan Armed Forces have the capability to detect Indian troop movements due to smaller distances and its increasing force multiplier technologies (AWACS, Reconnaissance etc.) that will give it early warning on enemy forces. For instance:

- Indian troop movements will be detected by Pakistani surveillance assets (AWACS, Radars, UAVs and satellites etc.).
- Rapid mobilisations of Pakistan's holding corps and defensive formations will done within 36–48 hours, this will be faster mobilisation than the Indian CSD can do.

- By the time the Indians actually transgress into Pakistani territory, the Pakistan Armed Forces will be well prepared to defend as they would have received significant time to bolster their defences and offensive capabilities.
- Due to a high level of synergy and interoperability between the Pakistan Army, PAF and the PN, tri-service air support for the troops fighting in the ground will be readily available.
- Force multiplier capabilities and advance technologies, would enhance Pakistan's defensive and offensive capabilities – increased situational awareness via network centric technologies, evolving UCAV/UAV capabilities ranging from surveillance and intelligence gathering to artillery fire correction, target acquisition and AGM capability would blunt an Indian attack and enable offensive manoeuvres into Indian territory.

Hence, Pakistan's New Concept of War Fighting (NCWF) is able to address the country's conventional capabilities as well as its nuclear. [94] Since Exercise 'Zarb-i-Momin' was conducted in 1989, there has been a radical change in Indian war fighting doctrine (Cold Start Doctrine) which Pakistan has been trying to counter from a conventional and nuclear aspect. Exercise Azm-e-Nau (New Resolve) had evolved into making the New Concept of War Fighting (NCWF) an updated doctrine for the Pakistan Armed Forces.

Pakistan MBT on exercise

---

[94] Pakistan claims to have developed NCWF to counter India's Cold Start Doctrine - http://defencenews.in/article/Pakistan-claims-to-have-developed-NCWF-to-counter-Indias-Cold-Start-Doctrine---Pak-Media-251068

Pakistani soldier on the western border

PAF F-16 dual-seat combat aircraft

PAF JF-17 Thunder Multi-role combat aircraft

PAF F-7P particpating in Azm-e-Nau (New Resolve) exercises

Pakistani army tanks advance in the Azm-e-Nau military exercises

Pakistani AH-1 Cobra Gunship Helicopter

Chapter 4: Pakistan's other External Security Perceptions

<u>Afghanistan, Iran and the Central Asian Republics (CARs)</u>

Pakistan's other threat perception after India, was its western neighbour Afghanistan. The Soviet Army's occupation of Afghanistan in December 1979 created an alarming situation for the security of Pakistan.[95] There were many dimensions to the problem; Pakistan was deeply concerned for a variety of reasons, such as the following:

(1)First, the Soviet control and its troops extended right up to Pakistan's Western border. Afghan and Soviet forces conducted raids against Afghan freedom fighters (mujahideen) bases inside Pakistan, Soviet and Afghan aircraft's intruded Pakistan airspace many times, and eventually resulted in many of them being shot down by the PAF. Overall the raids caused hundreds of casualties in Pakistan.[96]

(2)Secondly, Pakistan was faced for the first time in its history with the prospects of a two-front war. India from the East (its ally in the region) in collaboration with Soviet forces from the West.[97]

(3)Thirdly, there was a serious risk that Afghanistan was by no means the final destination of Soviet troops. Their aim was still the warm waters of the Arabian Sea, by advancing right through southern Pakistan. In such a scenario, of Soviet access to the warm waters, would also place Soviet influence and military power in close proximity to the

---

[95] Cordesman, op cit:80
[96] Chris Bishop, Encyclopaedia of Air Warfare-Volume 2, Aerospace Publishing Ltd, 1997, Pg143
[97] Walter Walker, The Next Domino?, The Covenant Publishing Ltd, 1980, Pg91

world's oil-supply sea-lanes from the Persian Gulf.[98]

This potential threat to the World's oil supply created considerable alarm in the Western capitals who depend on their entire way of life on the uninterrupted supply of oil from the Middle East.[99] Consequently the United States declared Pakistan a 'frontline state' against Soviet aggression and offered to reopen aid and military assistance deliveries. Other donors also rallied to Pakistan as it stood firm against Soviet blustering, hospitably received over 3 million Afghan refugees who poured across the borders, provided a conduit for weapons and other support, and gave a safe haven to the Afghan mujahideen. Billions dollars were spent to help the Afghan mujahideen fight the occupation forces, which eventually forced the USSR out of Afghanistan in 1989.[100]

However, Pakistan paid a price for its activities. The refugee burden created dangerous pressures within Pakistani society. Afghan and Soviet forces conducted raids against mujahideen bases inside Pakistan, and a campaign of terror bombings and sabotage in Pakistan's cities, guided by Afghan intelligence agents, caused hundreds of casualties.[101]

After the withdrawal of the Soviet troops from Afghanistan, Pakistan had expected a friendly regime in Afghanistan, which could provide strategic depth and quell nationalist ethnic forces in Pakistan and also of it desire to maintain economic ties with Central Asia Republics.

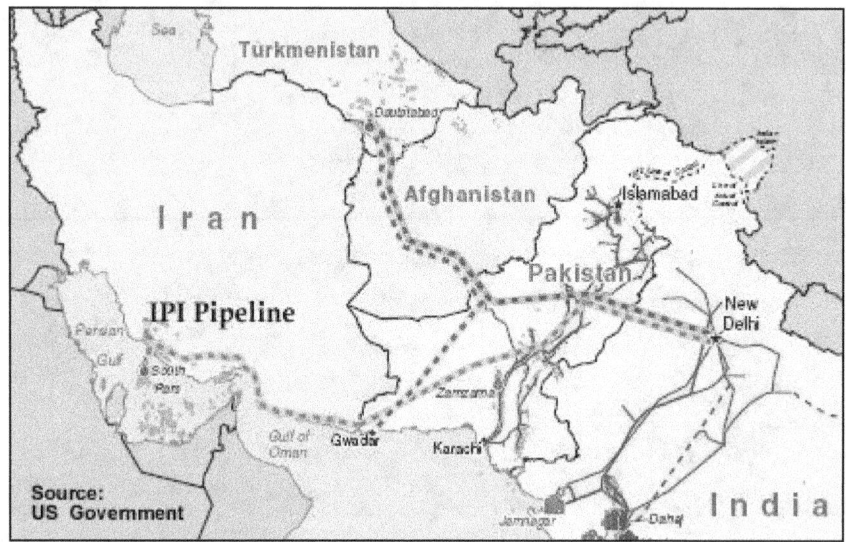

With a virtual scramble for the markets of the Central Asian Republics (CAR) from the developed countries, Pakistan hoped it could provide the needed outlet for the landlocked CARs through Afghanistan, by seeking a trade route through Afghanistan to Central Asia. In addition, Pakistan also hoped that a natural gas pipeline from Turkmenistan (UNOCOL) could be built through Afghanistan not only to meet its increasing domestic demand but also help the former to export gas to other countries.

However, under Prime Minister Rabbani's administration of Afghanistan, Pakistan's hope of developing a trade route to Central Asia was being shattered. Pakistan had supported Rabbani's rival, Hekmatyar. When Rabbani took power in Afghanistan, Pakistan declared the Rabbani government illegitimate; Pakistan's embassy in Kabul was later attacked and closed by Rabbani supporters. India, Russia and Iran began to forget close relations with the Rabbani administration (Indian involvement with the Rabbani government, was of specific concern); and Pakistan found itself secluded from much of Afghanistan.[102]

In 1994, Pakistan helped create the fundamentalist Taliban (Islamic students) faction, which was largely recruited from Afghan students attending religious schools in Pakistan. As the situation between Afghanistan and Pakistan deteriorated, Pakistan seems to have increased its assistance to this group.

By 1999, in a series of attacks that incorporated the use of armour, aircraft and perhaps Pakistani advisors, the estimated 40,000-50,000 strong Taliban was successful in expanding its control to encompass 90 percent of Afghanistan, to include securing Kabul in September 1996. As of the end of 1999, the three main anti-Taliban groups (generally representing the Tajik, Uzbek and Shiite-oriented factions) are holding northern Afghanistan under Rabbani, who still enjoys recognition by Iran, India and Russia as head of the legitimate government of Afghanistan.

---

[98] Walker, op cit:23

[99] Ibid

[100] Hewitt, op cit:104

[101] Walker, op cit:67

[102] Imtiaz Bakhari, The beginning of another 'Great Game'?, Jang Publishers Ltd, September 26, 1998, Pg10

The impressive military advances by the Taliban during the summer of 1998 and the disintegration of the northern alliance seemed to vindicate the approach adopted by Pakistani Policy-makers in Afghanistan.[103]

At last, it appeared that Pakistan's long-standing policy of supporting a Taliban front to establish a friendly, if not client, regime in Afghanistan that could provide strategic depth and quell its own ethnic (Pashtun and Baluchi) nationalist forces in Pakistan had borne fruit. However, the successful results achieved by the Taliban had resulted in increasing tensions with neighbouring Iran, which could lead to further conflict in the area.

In 2001 the US had invaded Afghanistan as part of its 'war on terror' operation. Over 40 countries, including all NATO members. The aim was to dismantle Al-qaeda and remove the Taliban from power. The Taliban were quickly defeated in the initial invasion but later reorganized and launched an insurgency against the Afghanistan government and ISAF forces in 2003. The conflict in Afghanistan also spilled into Pakistan's borders and its Tribal areas, causing widespread security issues for Pakistani Government and its Armed Forces.[104]

US troops began to increase from 2009-2011, reaching approximately over 100,000 and another 40,000 foreign troops under ISAF. Hence a total number of 140,000 troops were engaged with the rebel forces in Afghanistan. On the 1st May 2011, US Navy SEALS had allegedly killed Osam bin Laden in Abbotabad, Pakistan and in May 2012 an exit strategy was endorsed by NATO forces and many troops were withdrawn. By 2017 there were over 13,000 troops remaining in Afghanistan to support the Afghanistan Government. The War in Afghanistan is currently the longest war in United States history. Many thousands of people have been killed in Afghanistan – including over 4,000 ISAF soldiers and contractors, 15,000 Afghan security forces and over 31,000 civilians.[105]

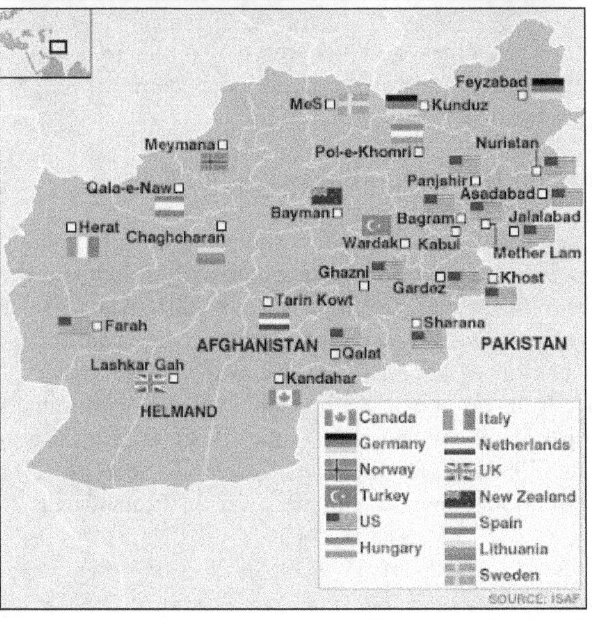

Despite the massive amount of military and economic aid that the US and its allies have poured into Afghanistan – it has not achieved the results it had desired. Afghanistan continues to be an unstable country with no signs of the conflict ending. The Taliban forces are thought to be occupying 40-70% of the country. The Pakistani government has rebuffed on many occasions by the US and Afghanistan governments accusation that Pakistan is giving sanctuary to the Taliban forces in its own country – Pakistan has stated that if the Taliban occupy more than 40% of Afghanistan, then they do not require any sanctuaries. Pakistan has suggested to Afghanistan and the US to clean its own 'house' up before making false accusations. If the US and its military might cannot stabilize Afghanistan and defeat the Taliban, then it's not fair if Pakistan is made to be the scapegoat for their inadequacies and failures.

---

[103] Ibid

[104] Walsh, Eric (2017). Trump speaks with Afghan leader, U.S. commander calls for more troops'. Reuters.

[105] Crawford, Neta (August 2016). 'Update on the Human Costs of War for Afghanistan and Pakistan, 2001 to mid-2016' (PDF).

According to the BBC news, **"Taliban fighters, whom US-led forces spent billions of dollars trying to defeat, are now openly active in 70% of Afghanistan. Months of research across the country shows that the Taliban now control or threaten much more territory than when foreign combat troops left in 2014".** [106]

Pakistan's relationship has been tense on many occasions, especially with the presence of Indian security forces in Afghanistan – who are here on the pretext of helping and developing Afghanistan. Pakistan's see the Indians as opening another front on its western border and supporting terrorist militant groups such as the TTP and other anti-

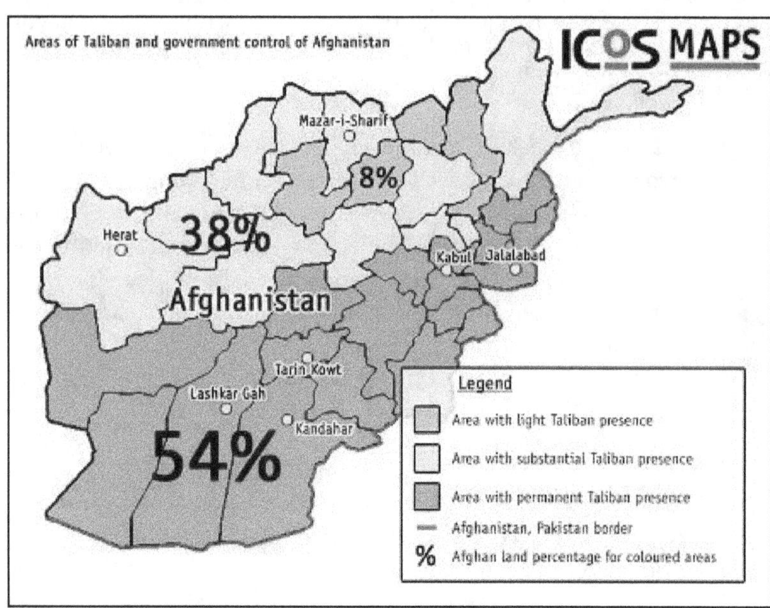

Pakistan affiliates. Border clashes have on numerous occasions contributed to more tense relationship with Pakistan. The border fence that Pakistan is putting up with Afghanistan will reduce the number of militants and terrorists to enter Pakistan's porous borders. Pakistan has stated that to end the conflict in Afghanistan has to be a political solution – talking with the Taliban. Afghanistan President Ashraf Ghani on 28 February 2018 has stated, **"that Kabul is ready for talks with Pakistan, adding that they want to forget the past and start a new chapter".** He further said, **"the peace process and a ceasefire must be agreed upon and that Taliban must be declared a political group".** This is something that Pakistan has been trying to convince the US and Afghan governments that to end the conflict can only happen via a political solution.[107]

With US as being the sole global superpower and with the support of the largest and powerful global military alliance, NATO – the war in Afghanistan has come to a stalemate. This frustration and for the US it has become its longest war ever, it has unfortunately tried to scapegoat Pakistan for its own failures.[108]

Pakistan and US Relations (America's War on Terror and its Impact on Pakistan)[109]

President Donald Trump and his administration has threatened tougher action in Afghanistan and had accused Pakistan of not 'doing enough' to contain the threat in Afghanistan. His remark on Twitter in January 2018 showed his hostility with Pakistan not doing enough to contain the conflict in Afghanistan. Afghanistan has been America's longest war so far – over 17 years of conflict since its 'war on terror' campaign. Pakistan was initially coerced into the 'war on terror' by the US - the Bush administration threatened to bomb Pakistan "back to the stone age" after the September 11 attacks if the country did not cooperate with America's war on Afghanistan. [110]

---

[106] Taliban threaten 70% of Afghanistan, BBC finds (January 2018) - http://www.bbc.co.uk/news/world-asia-42863116

[107] Want to forget past and start new chapter with Pakistan, says Ashraf Ghani - https://www.geo.tv/latest/184054-want-to-start-a-new-chapter-with-pakistan-ashraf-ghani

[108] INDEX ON AFGHANISTAN, NATO FAILURE: A WINTER'S TALE, PART II - http://indexresearch.blogspot.co.uk/2008/03/index-on-afghanistan-nato-failure.html

[109] http://www.politifact.com/truth-o-meter/article/2017/aug/21/donald-trumps-afghanistan-address-fact-checked/

[110] Bush threatened to bomb Pakistan, says Musharraf - https://www.theguardian.com/world/2006/sep/22/pakistan.usa

According to the former president, General Pervez Musharraf, the message was delivered by Richard Armitage (Assistant secretary of State) in conversations with Pakistan's intelligence director. He states the following, **"The intelligence director told me that (Mr Armitage) said, 'Be prepared to be bombed. Be prepared to go back to the stone age',"** [111] This shows the preparedness of a so called ally to coerce Pakistan – after 17 years of conflict in

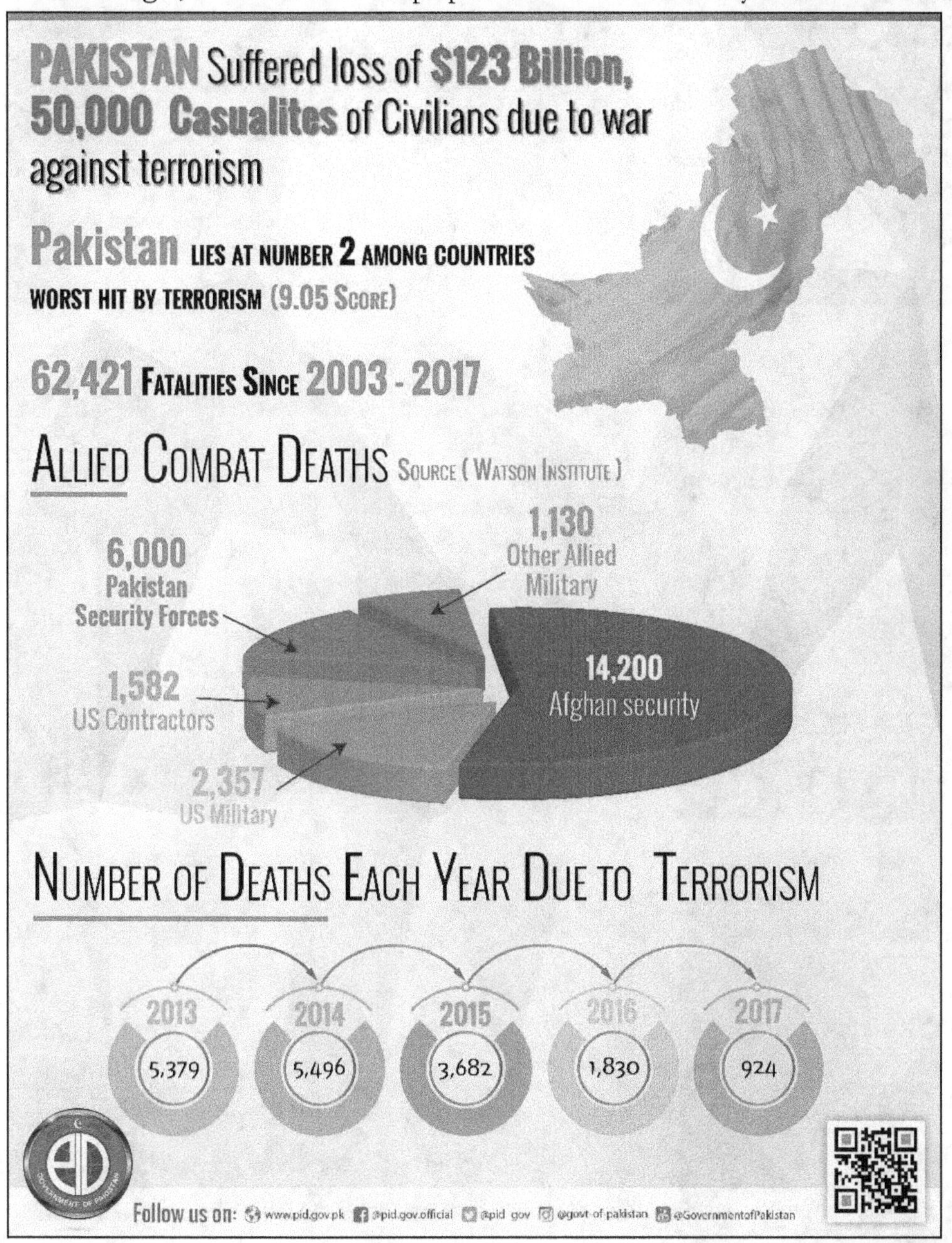

Afghanistan the US frustration has led it scapegoat Pakistan as the reason for the US and NATO's failure to defeat the Taliban in Afghanistan. Pakistan has allowed the use of its territory to supply US/NATO and other international troops in landlocked Afghanistan, silently accepted American drones over its airspace, and co-operated with Western intelligence agencies against some terrorist groups like Al Qaeda. However, this has not been enough for the US – the US has threatened and rebuked Pakistan on a number of occasions and had established closer ties to Pakistan's nemesis India.

Pakistan has suffered from numerous drone strikes and has lost the largest number of civilians in America's war on terror. Pakistan lost over 50,000 civilians[112] in war on terror, and billions of dollars of economic loss. The US led war on terror has caused considerable resentment across the world and primarily in Pakistan – especially in the light of ingratitude from the US and its allies. The war on terror has led to many terrorist activities taking place and much loss of life. The Pakistan armed forces had waged a counter-insurgency war against terrorist outfits who were being supported by external powers to weaken and divide Pakistan.

---

[111] Ibid

[112] Pakistan lost 50,000 Civilians - https://tribune.com.pk/story/1599831/1-pakistan-lost-50000-civilians-war-terror/

Drone strikes by the US has caused widespread loss of innocent civilian lives and has led to widespread protests in Pakistan, resulting in tense relationship with Pakistan.

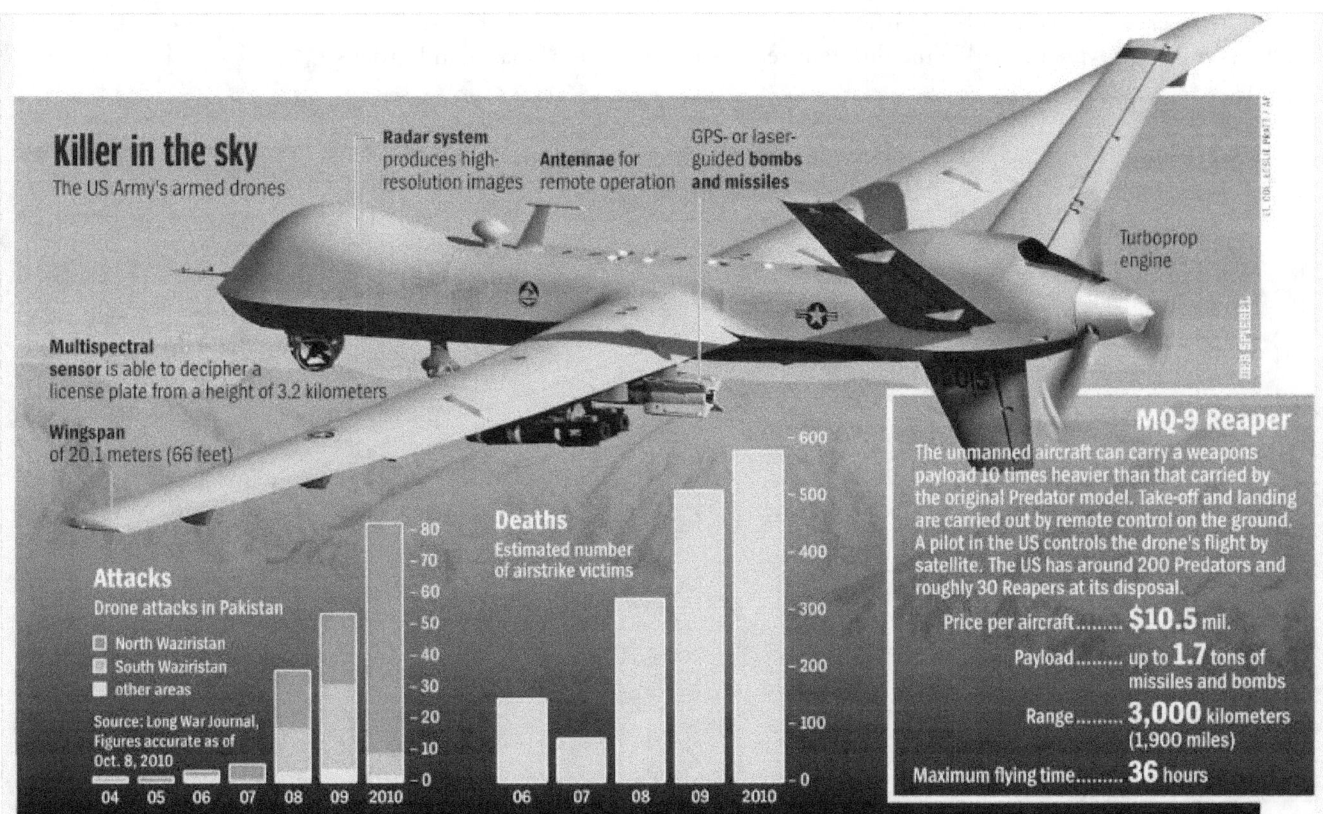

The intense and reckless drone attacks on the borders of Pakistan has contributed to further instability in the region. The loss of civilian lives due to drone attacks has caused a lot of ill feelings towards the US and its allies. The immoral weapon has been aptly used in developing countries and has violated numerous countries sovereignty.

Pakistan has stated that will shoot down any drone that violates its territory. The Pakistan Air Force (PAF), Air Chief Marshal Sohail Aman has warned that Pakistan would shoot down US drones if they violate its airspace.[113]

Operation Zarb E Azab (Counterinsurgency)

Pakistan has faced major threats to its security from terrorist incidents as a result of the conflict in Afghanistan (war on terror) – terrorist armed with heavy weapons and supported by foreign powers to cause maximum chaos and destruction of mainland Pakistan, with the aim of breaking the state of Pakistan as it is.

Pakistan undertook operation Zarb E Azb and all three services of the armed forces of Pakistan played significant part in eradicating the terrorist threat. The PAF was employed to take out key strategic terrorist hideouts, but was wary of causing collateral damage. The PAF utilized its assets and precision strikes were initiated by the PAF fighter jets – F-16 Falcons, Mirages and JF-17 Thunders took part in the attacks on terrorist positions.

113

This was the first time that the JF-17 thunder was employed in combat roles – Turkish, Chinese and USA electronic pods were used (Sniper, Aselpod etc.). The PAF's JF-17's have probably used unguided and guided precision munitions – Laser guided bombs (LGB) may have been paired with the Chinese WMD-7 targeting pod. The various militants positions were tracked in the different regions close to the Afghanistan border.

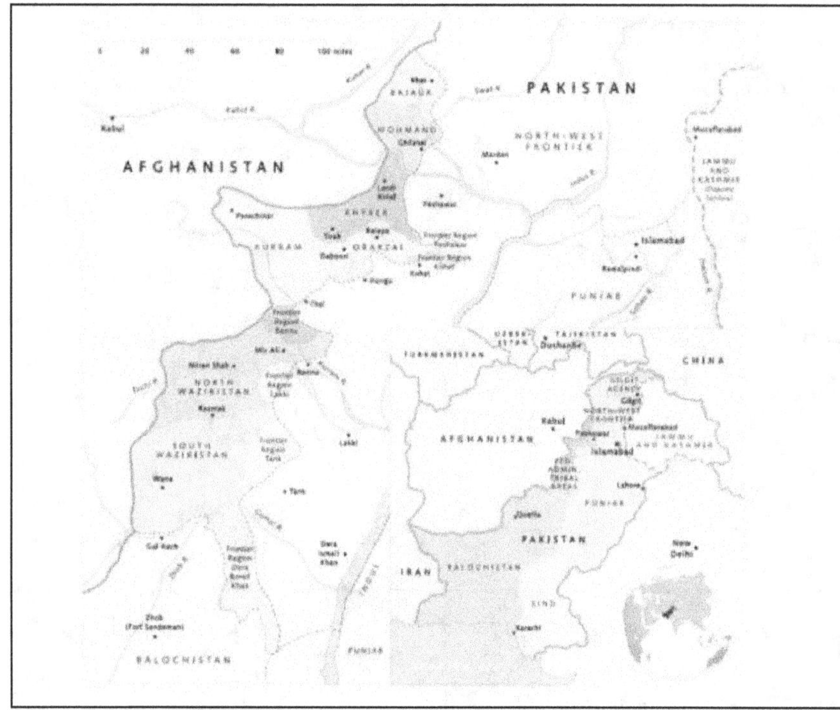

JF-17 with precision munitions are thought to have taken part on some of the attacks on terrorist positions in conjunction with PAF F-16s.

The aircrafts have operated with other air platforms in the PAF's inventory, such as its AWACS type aircraft and specially modified transport aircraft, such as the C130 Hercules aircraft.
The C130 were modified with FLIR equipment to track and locate enemy positions. They were working on an Intelligence, Surveillance and reconnaissance (ISR) mission.

The C130 would provide the target information and the PAF's jet fighters (including the JF-17) would partake in the strike missions.[114]

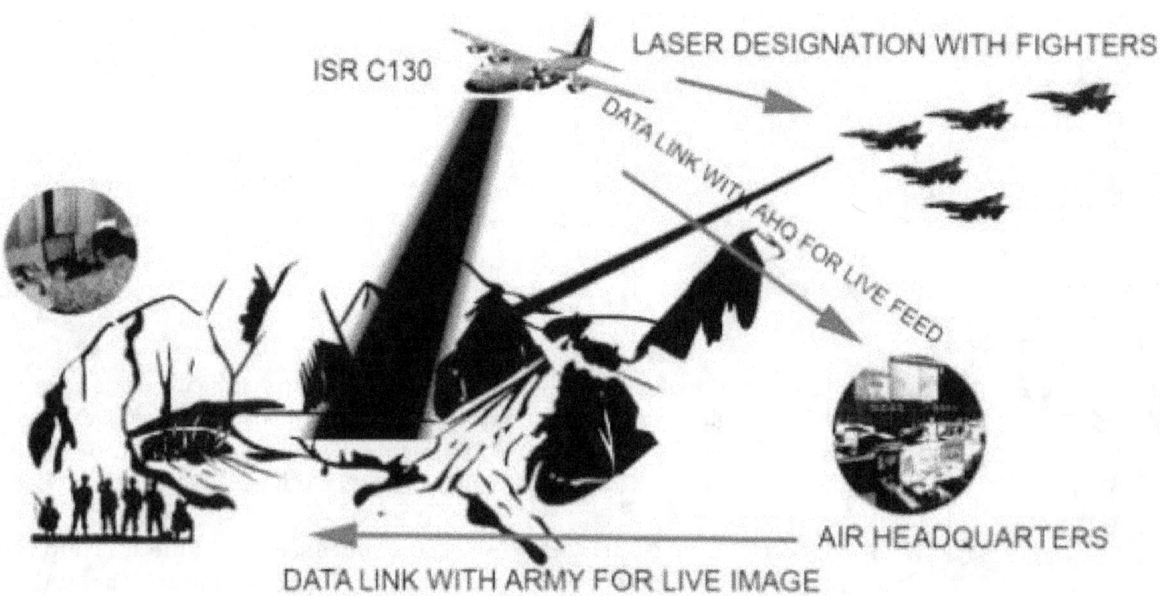

---

[114] http://www.paf.gov.pk

The combination of supporting aircraft with fighter aircraft has enabled the PAF to play a vital role in reducing and eliminating the serious threats to Pakistan's integrity. The terrorist violence has been significantly reduced as compared to many years back when the attacks were done on a daily basis with a collosal loss of life and property. The JF-17 has taken part in many exercises in Pakistan and in China where its capability has been refined and made better after evaluations.[115]

A pair of armed PAF JF17 on a training sortie (Promotional video) PAF[116]

Drone (UAV) shot down

On 19 June 2017 an unmanned aerial vehicle (UAV) was shot down and wreckage was recovered by Pakistani security forces.[117] The JF-17 had achieved its first aerial kill, when the UAV was shot down by an air-to-air missile. An Iranian drone was on unauthorized flight/spying mission deep inside Pakistani airspace and a message was sent out that this would not be tolerated. [118] According to Pakistan Government officials, the unmanned aircraft was shot down by a JF-17 in the Parom area of Panjgur district after it ventured into Pakistani airspace on a spying mission.

Combat missions

All in all, Pakistan has been aggressively using air power in its military campaign against terrorists in the country's restive northwestern regions along Afghanistan's border. The PAF combat aircraft in conjunction with the Pakistan Army's gunship helicopters have been pounding terrorist positions across the restive borders with Afghanistan.

---

[115] http://www.paf.gov.pk
[116] https://www.youtube.com/watch?v=ZthdDd1Qj6A
[117] https://theaviationgeekclub.com/jf-17-scores-first-aerial-kill-iranian-drone/
[118] https://www.dawn.com/news/1340703

As can be seen, the JF-17 had played vital roles in its own going security operations against terrorist outfits – such as Raad-ul-Fisaad and Zarab- i- Azab.[119] There is no doubt that as the aircraft matures and is incrementally upgraded, it will take on more responsibilities with a potent air defence and strike abilities.[120]

Currently Pakistan has been successful in eradicating terrorism in Pakistan and have improved the internal security of the country.

Pakistan- US Relations

Pakistan's relations with the US appeared to be weakening following its nuclear tests and subsequent US missile attack on Afghanistan. The US has indicated that it expects Pakistan to unconditionally sign the CTBT and withdraw its support of the Taliban. On the other hand, Pakistan is anxious for the US to relax its punitive sanctions imposed after the May 28th tests. However, the US attacks on Osama bin Laden raised further Pakistani concerns regarding the methodology of the United States war on terrorism.[121] All in all, the US pressures on Pakistan and the attempt to cause instability in Pakistan has resulted in ties being at the very low end. Drone strikes, military and economic blackmail and a threat to Pakistan on a terrorist list has not helped with the relationship. The fear for Pakistan is a new assertive and Zionist influenced US trump administration and its close nexus with Israel and India – is seen as a recipe for potential conflict. Pakistan's fear of a nexus of powerful non-Muslim countries are trying

---

[119] https://nation.com.pk/30-Dec-2017/paf-achieved-big-successes-in-2017

[120] https://warisboring.com/this-is-the-ultimate-mig-21-715bb9297261#.9t4jtsv29

[121] Umer Farooq, Striking Consequences, Janes Defence Weekly, September, 1998, Pg23

to divide and destroy Pakistan under the pretext of the 'War on Terror'. Pakistan is keeping a good watch on the ways that the destruction of Muslim majority countries have taken place, Such as in Iraq, Libya, Syria etc.

A fully armed US MQ-9 Reaper UCAV

US Drone strike on militants on the Afghanistan and Pakistan border

US Accused of 'Violating Pakistani Sovereignty' in Taliban Drone Strike

Drone strikes killed more civilians than publicly acknowledged' – UN investigator[122]

---

[122] https://www.rt.com/news/un-drones-report-afghanistan-us-366/

Iran and Pakistan's relationship:

In the early 1990s, key Pakistani elements entertained hopes of establishing a strategic alliance with Iran and other regional Islamic states to offset and expected tilt of the United States toward India. However, relations between Pakistan and Iran have become strained recently, mainly due to political, economical and ideological differences.

Pakistan's political interests were clear-having served as the vanguard of US-funded support for the Afghan mujahideen against the Soviet-backed regime; it justifiably felt that the time for payback was not far. This meant, for Pakistani policy-makers, an Afghan government that was closely aligned to Islamabad and composed primarily of Pashtun military leaders, notably Gulbuddin Hekmatyar, who had been the chief recipient of military and political support through Pakistan during the Jihad years. Pakistan's traditional political interests in a friendly Afghanistan – strategic depth and curbing Pashtun secessionism – were reinforced by the emergence of energy-rich countries in Central Asia.[123]

Iranians border patrol

Iran has felt alienated by the way in which each country has perceived its respective interests as being mutually opposed in Afghanistan. The degree of antagonism has been heightened after the Taliban's military advances in the north and most recently by the indiscriminate killings of Iranian diplomats as well as Shia civilians in Hazara. Iran has historically been uncomfortable with Pakistan's pro-American orientation and its willingness to accept American

---

[123] Rahimullah Yusufzai, Taliban's Achilles Heels, Jang Publishers Ltd, November, 1998, Pg10

foreign policy for the region.[124]

Since the withdrawal of Soviet troops from Afghanistan, Pakistan has sought to increase its influence in the Central Asian Region. The region has large reserves of oil and natural gas and is therefore of vital strategic importance to both Pakistan and Iran. The natural route to the Central Asian region for outsiders would be through Iran. However, there is some Iranian resentment at the way it feels outside countries are choosing to go through either Pakistan or Afghanistan as the chosen route.

Pakistan, on the other hand, has lobbied for Turkmenistan's oil and gas pipelines to pass through Afghanistan into Pakistan, providing vital low-cost power to Pakistani industry, whilst contributing to its economic development. With a virtual scramble for the markets of the Central Asian Republics (CAR) from the developed countries, Pakistan thought it could provide the needed outlet for the landlocked CAR through Afghanistan. A Tashkent-Karachi transportation link and the enterprise of its businessmen is central to Pakistan's CAR policy.[125]

There has been a growing suspicion in Pakistani that Iran was actively involved in agitating Pakistan's Shia community. Relations between Iran and India have improved recently, including formal co-operative arrangements between the two to open trade routes through Iran to the Central Asian republics. This agreement put those states into direct competition with Pakistan for providing a Central Asia outlet to the sea.[126]

Iran is unhappy with the extreme Islamic radicalism of the Sunni Taliban, whilst at the same time, the Shia dominant area of Herat has looked to Iran for assistance against the strict Taliban governance of the region. For its part, Iran has been training and equipping an 8,000- strong Shia dominated Afghan group in eastern Iran, apparently in an effort to prepare the group to retake the Herat area. The accompanying tensions have caused some very discreet 'sabre-rattling' between Iran and Pakistan, whilst the two countries have maintained a public image of apparent friendly relations.[127] Iranian and Pakistani tensions have risen up sporadically along their border due to smugglers and terror related activities. The tussle that the Iranians and Saudi's have over gaining the leadership/influence in the Muslim world has led these two countries promoting tensions amongst the Pakistani population on sectarian grounds. Furthermore, Iran's strong ties with India and the development of the Chabahar port is seen as undermining Pakistan.

Indian spy Kulbhushan Jadhav

An Indian senior Naval officer was caught in Pakistan's Baluchistan province – he was responsible for causing a lot of sunversive and terrorist activities in Pakistan. He had a passport and Visa from Iran, "Pakistan has alleged that Jadhav, who was running a business in Chabahar, was caught in Pakistan for subversive activities in Baluchistan".[128] Pakistan is concerned that the the Indo-Iranian-Afghanistan nexus is being used against its legitimate interests.

---

[124] Anthony Davies, Will Iran choose War?, Janes Defence Weekly, 23 September, 1998, Pg22

[125] Bokhari, op cit:10

[126] Davies, op cit:22

[127] Ibid

[128] Iran probing Jadhav case, says Ambassador Gholamreza Ansari - http://indianexpress.com/article/india/india-news-india/india-spy-pakistan-kulbhushan-jadhav-iran-balochistan-2764703/

Pakistan and the Indo-Israel Military Nexus

Indian Prime minister Modi and Israeli Prime minister Netanyahu.

Another area of Pakistan security concern is the improving military ties between India and Israel. Since formal ties were established in 1992, Israeli military exports to India have grown to over $150 million a year. From the period 2012-2016 Israeli firms sold up to $1 billion a year in sales to India on average. In fiscal 2016-18, Israel is trying to sell the sophisticated Spike anti-tank missiles - if India goes through with this deal, Israel will be for the first time the largest arms supplier to India.[129] The defence co-operation includes sophisticated pilot-less drones, night vision equipment and extending to the nuclear, ballistic missile targeting systems and spy satellite technology.[130]

India-Israel ties increased military ties and the sales of sophisticated items to the Indian armed forces has caused a lot of concern to Pakistan. Force multiplier Israeli technologies have been sold to India and agreements in development projects of military related equipment has also increased. Pakistan is especially worried about the sale of the state-of-the-art Arrow anti-missile system that gives India the potential to neutralize part of Pakistan's nuclear ballistic missile capability. In addition, the Phalcon Airborne Early Warning, Command and Control (AEW&C) system will give India the deep edge and capability to look deep into Pakistan's territory (it gives India the ability to easily detect the movement of Pakistan's combat aircraft). Also the co-development of the Barak Anti-missile system will gives the Indian Navy huge advantage in its defensive and offensive capability.[131]

Israel has viewed that Pakistani nuclear programme with a growing sense of alarm since the 1970s. It fears an 'Islamic Bomb' either being deployed to counter Israel's nuclear and conventional security over its Arab foes, or being transferred to an Arab country.[132] In 1981, Prime Minister Sharon of Israel indicated that the security of the Israeli entity included Pakistan.[133]

In the 1980s, there were reports in both the British and Indian media of Israel requesting Indian co-operation to bomb the Kahuta reactor in Pakistan. This would have involved the use of the Indian air base at Jamnagar near the Pakistan border as a possible refuelling stop. India reportedly declined the request due to the fear of a Pakistani retaliation on its own nuclear sites.[134] Moreover in 1991, Pakistan's Interior Ministry warned Parliament of another possible joint Israeli-Indian sabotage attempt at Kahuta, which is only 20km from the Srinagar capital of Indian-held Kashmir.[135]

According to the Indian weekly *'News Behind News'*, Major General Ivry, the second-in-command of the Israeli Defence Ministry, attempted another Israeli-Indian collaboration in 1995. He requested the use of Indian airbases at Jodhpur or Bhuj, on the basis of a *'common threat perception'*, in return for an Israeli package deal to India which included

---

[129] Israel likely to become India's largest arms supplier - https://www.hindustantimes.com/world-news/israel-likely-to-become-india-s-largest-arms-supplier/story-tZQFenVzYWzaQFnPqbznqM.html

[130] Yoel Cohen, India bomb test may affect Israel Relations, Jewish Chronicle, Publishers Jewish Chronical Newspaper Ltd, May 29, 1998, Pg3

[131] India-Israel Strengthened Nexus - http://hilal.gov.pk/index.php/layouts/item/2805-india-israel-strengthened-nexus

[132] Ibid

[133] Y. Ammar, The Kashmir Factor, Palestine Times, 9 October, 1991, Pg2

[134] Cohen, op cit:3

[135] Ammar, op cit:4

airborne warning and control systems (AWACS), remotely piloted vehicles (RPV), sophisticated radar jammers and specialised weapons, including parts of its own spy satellite technology. India turned down this package, which would almost certainly have raised fears of a Pakistani retaliation on India's own reactors.[136]

Of greater concern was Israeli-Indian nuclear co-operation. Dr Abdul Kalam, the architect of India's nuclear and ballistic missile programme, visited Israel several times, over a period of months between 1996-1997. Senior Israeli scientists also made several visits to India over the same period. The close ties between Dr Kalam and his Israeli counterparts have suggested parallels with Israel's secret co-operation with South Africa in at least one nuclear test in the late 1970s.[137]

Israeli US supplied F-16 multi-role combat aircraft

According to *The Washington Times,* Pakistan feared a combined Indo-Israeli pre-emptive air-strike as it conducted its first nuclear test on 28th May 1998, in the same way that Israeli combat aircraft destroyed Iraq's Osirak nuclear reactor in 1981.[138] An F-16 fighter-bomber was spotted twice in Pakistan's airspace just before the tests. The aircraft was assumed to be part of an Israeli strike-force, as India has no F-16 aircraft in its airforce. Pakistan, suspecting that Israeli jets were using Indian bases, made preparations to counter an air-strike by placing its air-force and missiles on high alert.[139]

Western defence experts did not rule out the possibility of an Indo-Israeli attack on Pakistan's nuclear facilities.

---

[136] News International, Israel offers India AWACS for Airbases as Part of 'Common Threat Perception', Jang Publishers Ltd, April 18, 1995, Pg1

[137] Christopher Walker, Israel's Helped India for 20 Years, The Times, Thursday June 4, 1998, Pg16

[138] Martin Sieff and Yoel Cohen, Pakistan Feared Israel's Strike during Nuclear test, Jewish Chronical, June 5, 1998, Pg3

[139] Christopher Walker and Michael Evans, Pakistan Feared Israeli Raid, The Times, Wednesday June 3, 1998, Pg3

According to Paul Beaver, of Jane's Information Group, the Israeli F-16s had been equipped with an advanced reconnaissance system to take high-altitude pictures of targets over a 50 miles radius. The high resolution pictures were capable of reading the lettering on the side of a truck parked at Pakistani nuclear facility.[140]

Israeli F-16 multi-role combat aircraft

Overall, Israel's offers of advance weapon systems, her help with India's nuclear and ballistic missile programme and also her assistance in providing expertise to India, to crush the uprising in Kashmir, point towards an Indo-Israeli nexus directed against Pakistan.[141]

Israeli US supplied Apache attack helicopter and Israeli soldiers on a patrol

---

[140] Ibid
[141] Ammar, op cit:2

Israeli F-15 Eagle combat aircraft

Pakistani MBT on exercise

<u>Pakistan and the Central Asian Republics</u>

Pakistan's support for the Taliban has somewhat alienated the same Central Asian countries with which it seeks closer economic relations. The leadership of these countries, compromised of former communist-cum nationalists, see a present and growing threat to their political power by Islamist forces. A Taliban take-over of Afghanistan could strengthen the Islamist opposition elements within their own countries. Additionally, a friendly and stable Afghanistan would open new commercial routes to these republics, thus decreasing the Russian hold on access to these markets.[142]

The withdrawal of Soviet troops was supposed to end the Afghan war and return the country to peace and a stable government. However, the former was not followed up by the latter, although the hope remained alive. This was the main reason for the recognition of the Taliban regime, which controls most of Afghanistan, much of it in areas to which it has traditionally belonged. The situation has not improved, partly due to Russian and Indian military assistance to the Uzbek and Tajik elements in the Northern sector of the country. Pakistan may have won the war in Afghanistan, but it has lost important friends in the region whose support was important both politically and economically. Pakistan is now surrounded by countries that are unfriendly, if not hostile to it. Afghanistan continues to be a source of concern to Pakistan and a threat to her western border.[143]

Pakistani soldiers on watch duties

Pakistani soldiers on exercises

---

[142] Bokhari, op cit:10
[143] Ibid

Chapter 5: Pakistan's Internal Security Threats

Pakistan's Internal Security Threats

Afghan Refugees

Pakistan seeks world support to repatriate 3m Afghan refugees

Afghan refugees have been crossing Pakistan's border ever since the Soviet invasion. This has continued despite the Taliban's control of most of Afghanistan. In 1988, the Afghan refugee count in Pakistan stood at over 3.5 million.[144] Besides creating ethno-demographic imbalances, the huge refugee influx has also posed social, economic and political challenges to Pakistan. The increase of crime, violence and the proliferation of arms in Pakistani society in the 1980s has been blamed directly on this refugee influx. The problems are compounded by the rise in political support from

---

[144] Mahnaz Ispahani, Pakistan: dimensions of insecurity, Brassey's, 1990, Pg44

certain parties, thus worsening domestic policy also. In Baluchistan, the refugee population has increased by 10-15 percent. The future for this province looks troubling; with the increase in Pushtoon refugees upsetting the ethnic balance between the Baluchis and the Pushtoons and making the Baluchis a minority in their own province.[145]

Proliferation of Arms

Coupled with the trafficking of drugs, the proliferation of small arms threatens the stability of both Pakistani society and the government. The root cause for small-arms proliferation lie in the arming of the Mujahideen forces by the US and Pakistan following the 1979 Soviet invasion. Illegal arms bazaars sprung up inside Pakistan, and the end of the Soviet occupation saw a glut of small arms on the local markets. A 'Kalashnikov' culture is now prevalent in the Sindh province and in the North-West Frontier. The availability of various anti-aircraft and anti-personnel weapons already has led to a virtual breakdown of law in Karachi.[146]

---

[145] Ibid
[146] Ispahani, op cit:26

Drug Cultivation and Trafficking

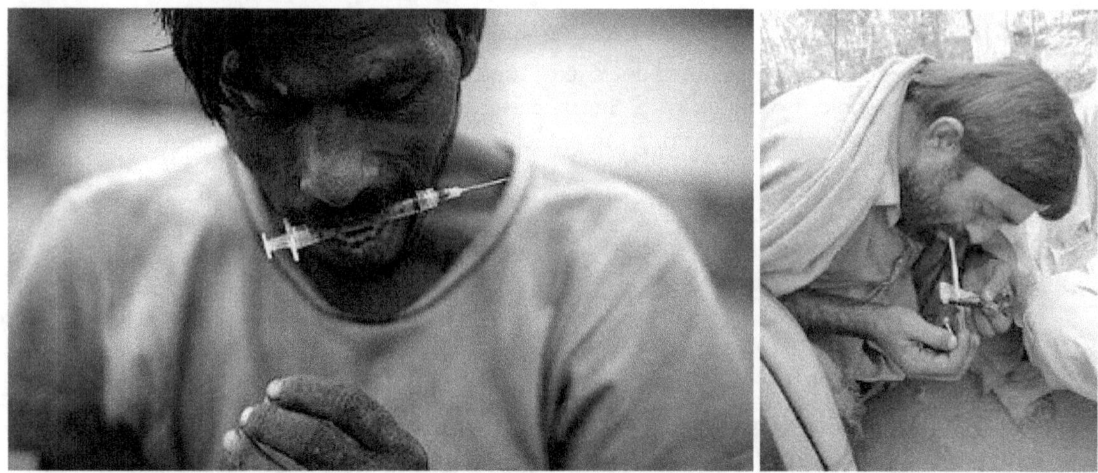

Drug use is endemic in Pakistan, but authorities are more concerned with heroin and opium

Pakistan currently enjoys a dubious reputation as a major producer and a transit point for drug trafficking. In 1997 Pakistan produced around 85 metric tons of opium, an estimated increase of 13.3 percent from the previous year. The security threat to the state by drug trafficking comes from three interrelated sections – internal drug cultivation and trafficking, external drug trafficking and increasing drug abuse within the state. Pakistan has approximately four million drug addicts. Drugs and drug money have come to play a dominant role in the power politics of Pakistan, with little of any reversal in this trend.[147]

Shia-Sunni Sectarian Violence

The problem of religious extremism in Pakistan stems mainly from outside factors such as Arab (Sunni) and Iranian

---

[147] Ibid

(Shia) rivalry. Sectarian violence has increasingly become commonplace between Pakistan's Sunni Muslim majority and its 15 percent Shia minority. Comparisons can be made with Protestant-Catholic relations in Northern Ireland, with similar hallmarks of conflict such as shootings, bomb incidents and beatings.[148]

Sindh Violence

CM Sindh approves extension in Rangers' special powers

Another majority threat to the internal security comes from the continuing violence in Sindh, especially in the economically important port city of Karachi. The major reason for the Karachi crisis comes from the alienated Mohajirs. Led by their powerful Mohajir Qaumi Movement (MQM), the Mohajirs have been fighting against successive Pakistani regimes in Karachi for more than a decade. Fighting has also taken place between the two fractions of the MQM – the Altaf and Haqiqi factions and also against non-mohajirs, as well as criminal gangs. Drug money and the Kalashnikov culture has led to an explosion in the number of violent deaths in Karachi. The situation threatens to destroy the social fabric across Pakistan. However, there appears to be no easy solution to the problem, as various successive regimes have swept the Karachi situation under the carpet in pursuit of their own political agendas.[149]

---

[148] Ispahani, op cit:20
[149] Ispahani, op cit:23

Ethnic Tensions

Punjab, with almost 60 percent of the population dominates almost all aspects of national life. This fact is resented by smaller ethnic groups, all of whom have at one or other have expressed dissent.[150] In the North-West Frontier Province, there is increasing dissent over the erosion of the province's autonomy, particularly after the renaming of the province as Pakhtoonkhwa, approved by the Provincial Assembly with a huge majority, was stonewalled by the federal government.

Rivalries dividing Punjab, Baluchistan, Sindh and North-West Frontier Province run so deep that their four regional governments cannot even agree on the Kalabagh Dam project, vital for future cross-Pakistan power and irrigation resources.

Pakistan's major problems regarding its various ethnic groups is the potential for their manipulation by outside powers.[151] For instance, Pakistan's Baluchi and Pashtun population overlap into neighbouring Afghanistan and the Baluchis also overlap into Iran.[152] In 1973, for instance, the Afghan government was successful in fomenting dissent in Baluchistan, in an effort to divert Pakistani manpower away from Afghanistan. Over 55,000 Baluchi personnel joined the struggle for an independent country (Greater Baluchistan).[153] Pakistan sent in over 70,000 troops to put down the separatist revolt, reportedly employing Iranian Huey Cobra helicopter gunships to quell disturbances there. Iran appeared to have been forthcoming in this initiative because it feared insurrection amongst its own Baluch ethnic groups.[154]

The PAF bombed suspected rebel positions, while Afghanistan threatened full-scale war in defence of the Baluch rebels. The rebels were defeated in 1974. The Afghan government had succeeded in the short-term by inflaming Baluchi drives for independence, thus diverting extra Pakistani troops to defend its least-defensible borders.[155]

To summarise – a friendly government in Kabul would resolve the Durand Line (border)[156] problem once and for all. This would also provide the much needed strategic depth against India, removing problems with its own Pakhtoon and Baluch populations – which an unfriendly Kabul could exacerbate – and allowing Pakistan to gain access to transportation networks in central Asia.[157]

---

150 Ispahani, op cit:22

151 Ispahani, op cit:26

152 General Walter Walker, The Next Domino?, The Covenant Publishing Co.Ltd, 1980, Pg63

153 Patrick Brogan, World Conflicts- Why and Where they are Happening, Bloomsbury Publishing Ltd, 1992, Pg238

154 Ibid

155 Ibid

156 Walker, op cit:63

157 Ibid

Economic and Financial Crisis

Pakistan faces an ongoing economic crisis, mainly due to the financial mismanagement of successive governments. With a population of over 200 million and a low literacy rate, poor health care and increasing drug abuse, Pakistan's economic challenges are formidable. Poverty remains a serious problem, with a significant percentage of the nation's budget accounting for debt servicing and defence expenditure.[158]

China and Pakistan – CPEC

Pakistan and China have both embarked on a massive $62 billion project in regards to developing the Gwadar sea port in Baluchistan's province of Pakistan. The China-Pakistan Economic Corridor (CPEC) may be a potential 'game-changer' project for both countries and give a vital boost to the economy. It gives both countries a number of advantages.[159]

---

[158] Ispahani, op cit:28

[159]Why Does India Want Pakistan And China's CPEC To Fail? - https://www.valuewalk.com/2017/02/india-cpec-china-

However, neighboring country is unhappy with this development and is trying its best to disrupt this multi-billion mega project. Also other countries, such as the USA and Afghanistan are also unhappy and are attempting to malign this project. All of Pakistan's adversaries are attempting to disrupt this project under various excuses and pretexts. India, USA, Afghanistan sees this as a threat to its security as this project would make Pakistan an economically stronger nation. A stronger economically Pakistan will be able to spend adequately on its defence needs and balance the security environment in the region.

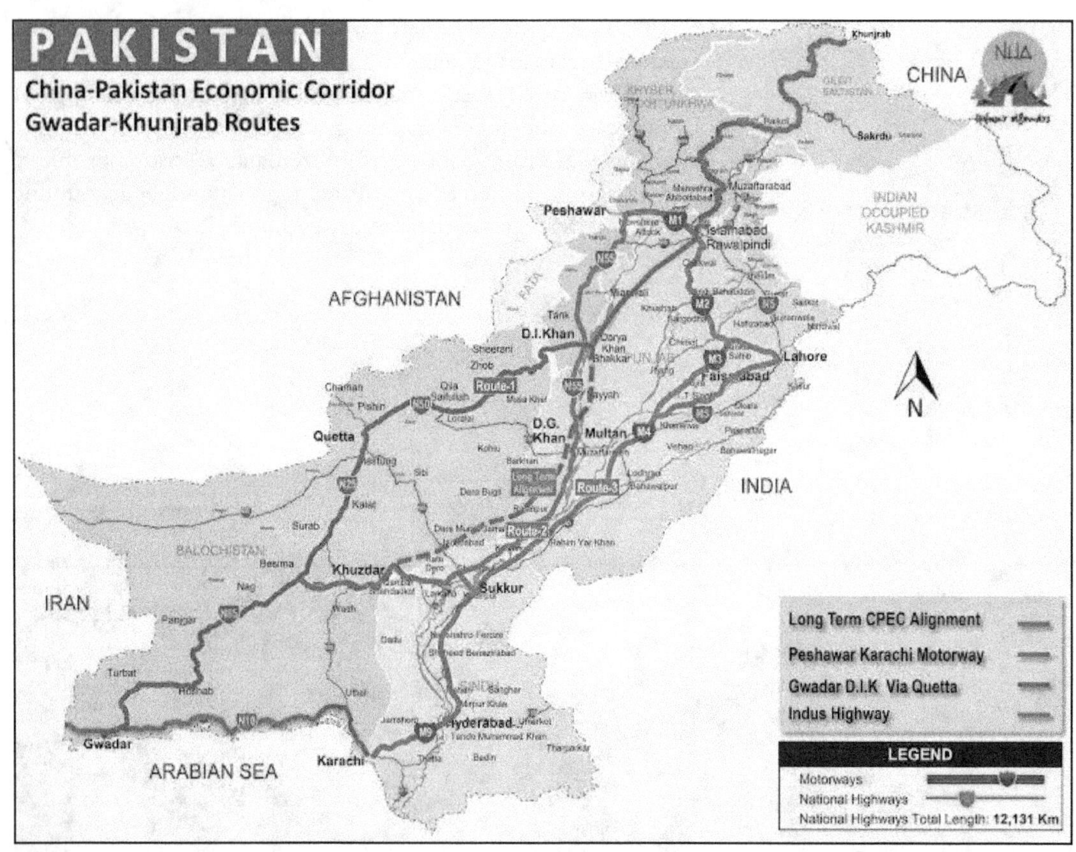

India has a number of concerns over this mega project - CPEC project has the potential to make Pakistan a stronger economical nation that would have more funds to spend on defence and would deprive India's of its regional hegemony ambition. It would also further enhance economic and defence ties between China and Pakistan.[160]

India is also worried that the CPEC project goes through the disputed territory of Kashmir of which a number of wars were fought. India has over 700,000 military personnel in their part of the Kashmir and is worried that the project would further internationalise the issue. The Muslim majority part of India's occupied Kashmir wants to join with Pakistan or seek independence. A UN plebiscite agreement to allow the Kashmiri people its choice has never been implemented by India as of fears the territory does not want to be joined by India.

A number of uprisings have taken place over the decades and there have been reports of genocide being taken place by Indian military forces. India is also worried about China's influence in the region and believes that CPEC will enable China to get direct access to the important Arabian Sea and also Chinese military presence in the area.

---

pakistan-fail/

[160] http://www.truthbykbaig.com/2016/07/the-realities-linked-with-opposition-of.html

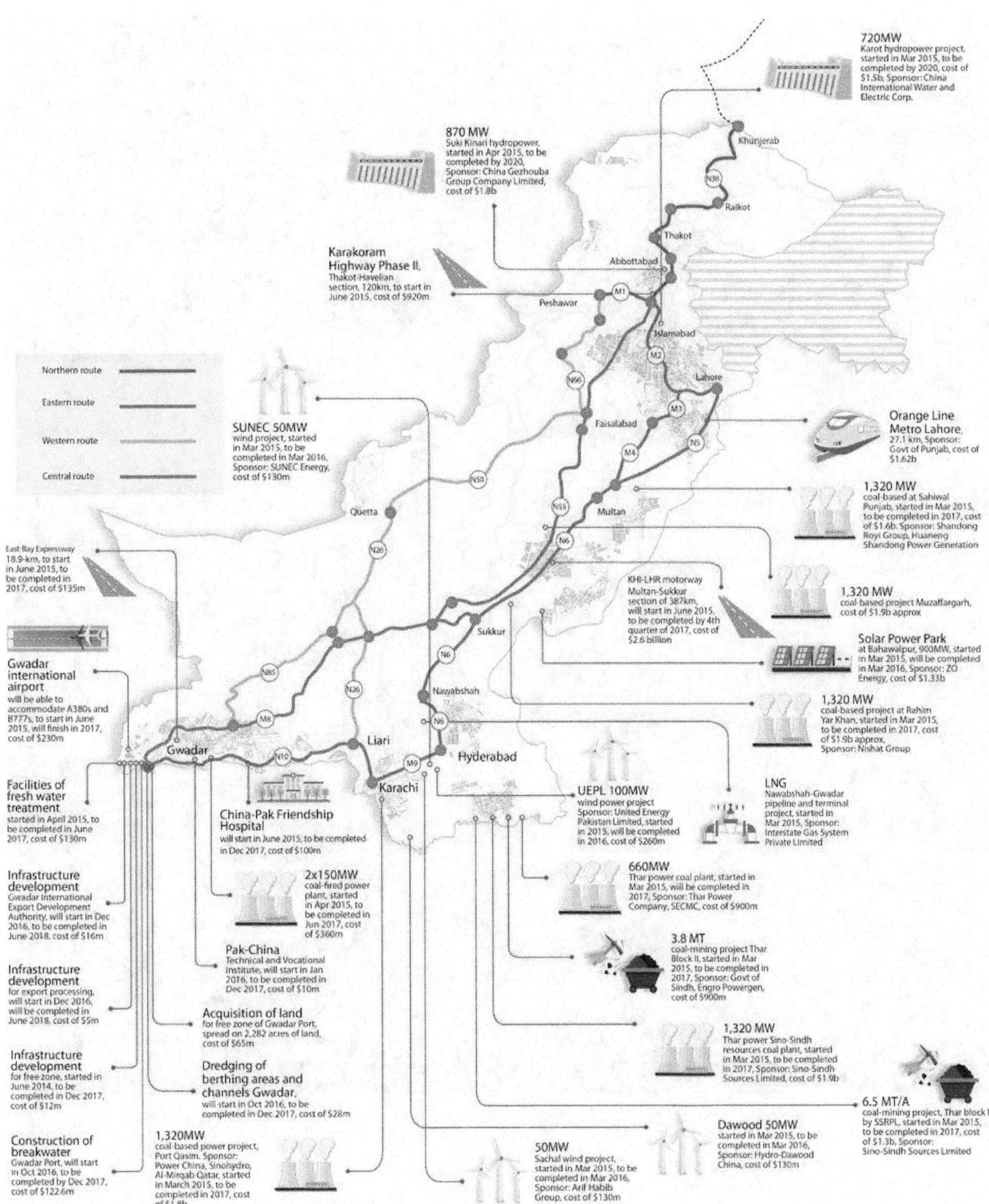

For Pakistan, it has a number of countries that views CPEC with suspicion and are willing to sabotage this project via a number of acts such as abetting and sponsoring terrorism in the Baluchistan province. To safeguard this, Pakistan is creating a 15,000-20,000 CPEC security force to protect the project.

Development of Gwadar port in Pakistan

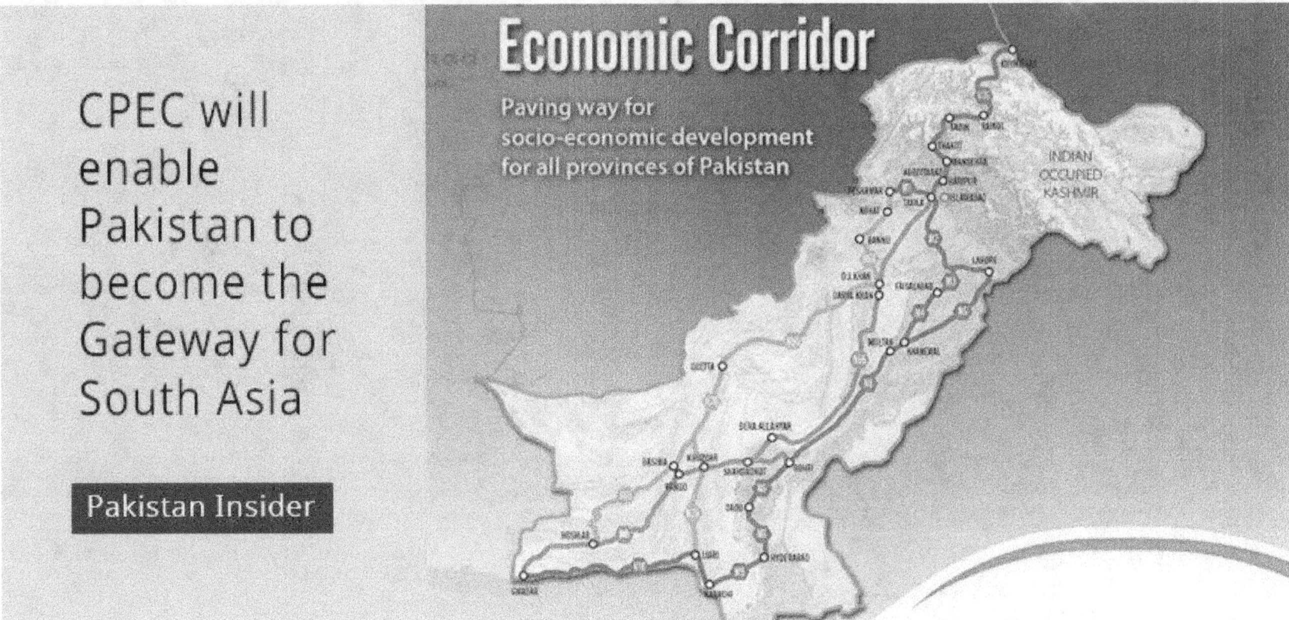

Pakistani soldier providing security against foreign sponsored terrorist attacks in Gwadar Port

Operation Zarb-e-Azb - More than 2700 terrorists killed

Pakistani and Chinese troops on exercise

Soldiers deployed for security of CPEC

Chapter 6: Regional Defence Spending and Weapons Procurement

Introduction

A sharp increase in the military budget of Asian countries has continued despite the negative impact of the global financial crisis. The nations in this region have procured sophisticated 'state of the Art' weapons, with an emphasis of key 'game changing' items in the region – modern submarines, ships, aircraft and long range anti-ship missiles. There is a fear that the region is sliding into an arms race due to the simmering differences amongst themselves. One countries purchase of weapons has given the impetus for a rival to obtained further arms. This increase in regional insecurity in Asia has resulted in the increase in military expenditure.

As the economic development in the region continues, more money has been allocated for safeguarding their respective interests.

Global Military Budget (regional 2016)

Total defence spending in 2016 – 1,504,167 billion[161]

---

[161] Chapter six: Asia. (2017). *The Military Balance, 117*(1), 237-350.

Table 1

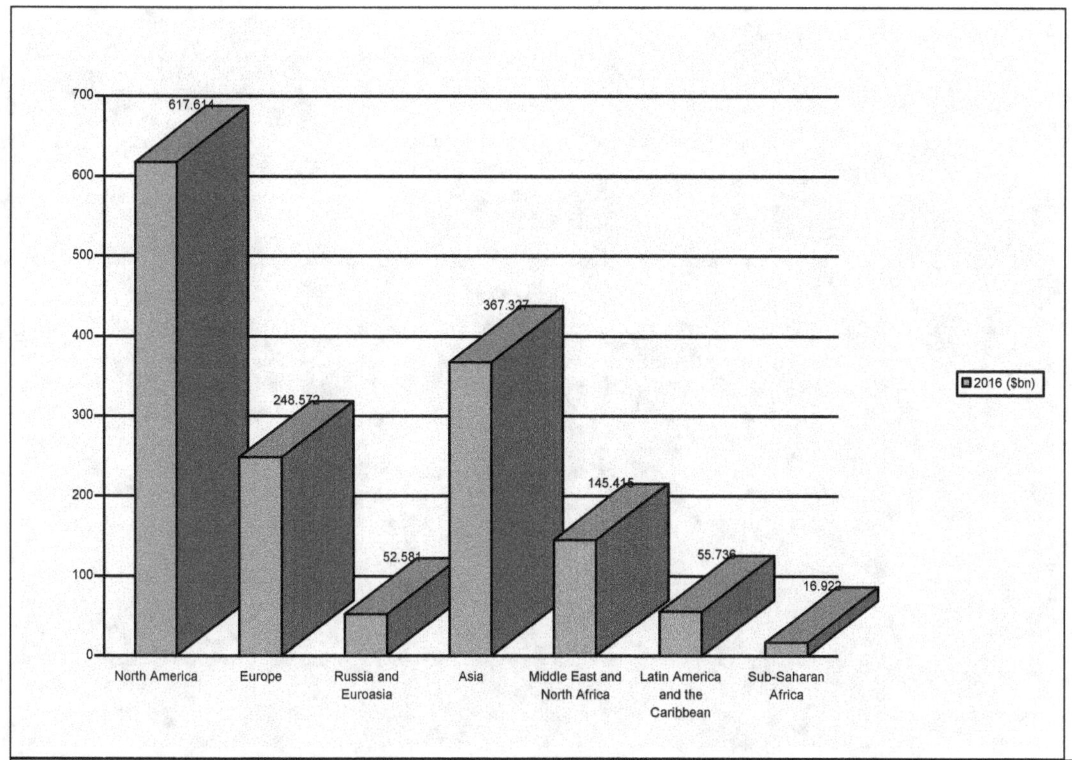

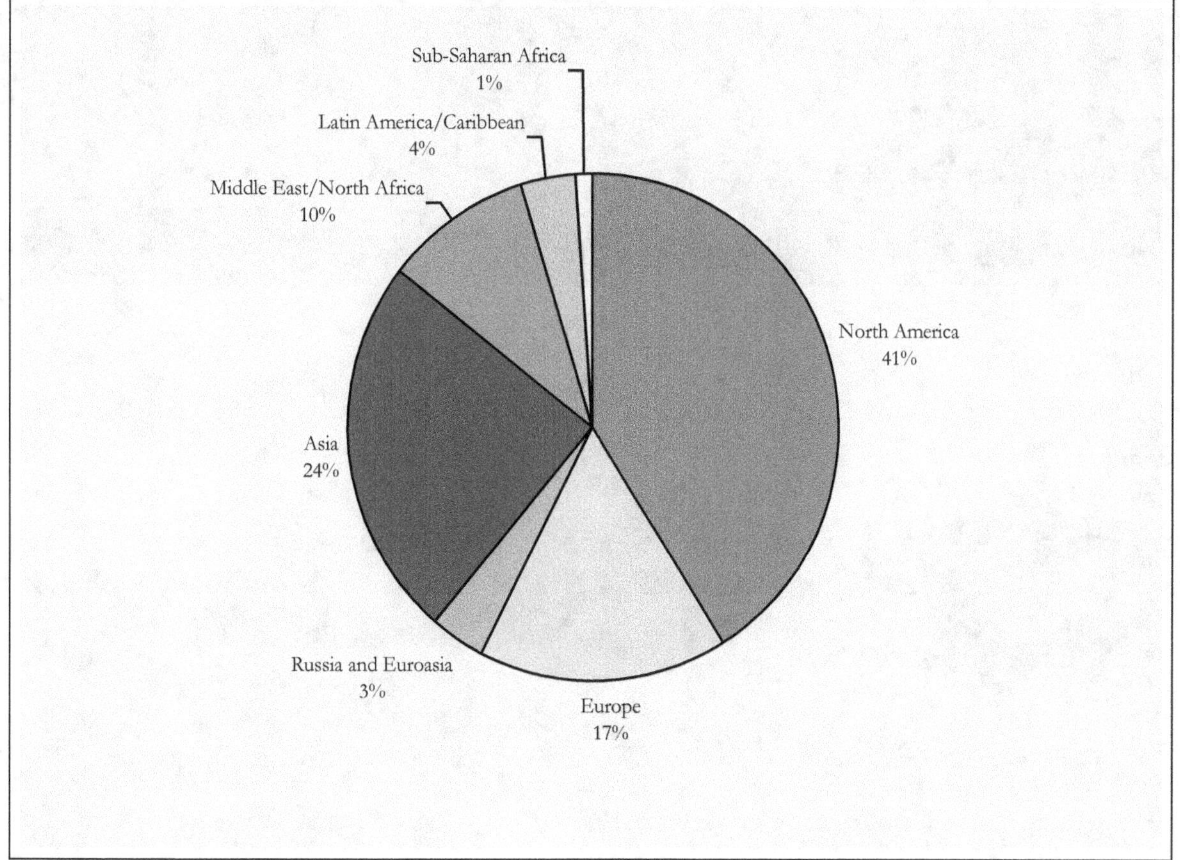

Global Military Budget (% 2016)

Pakistan's neighbours

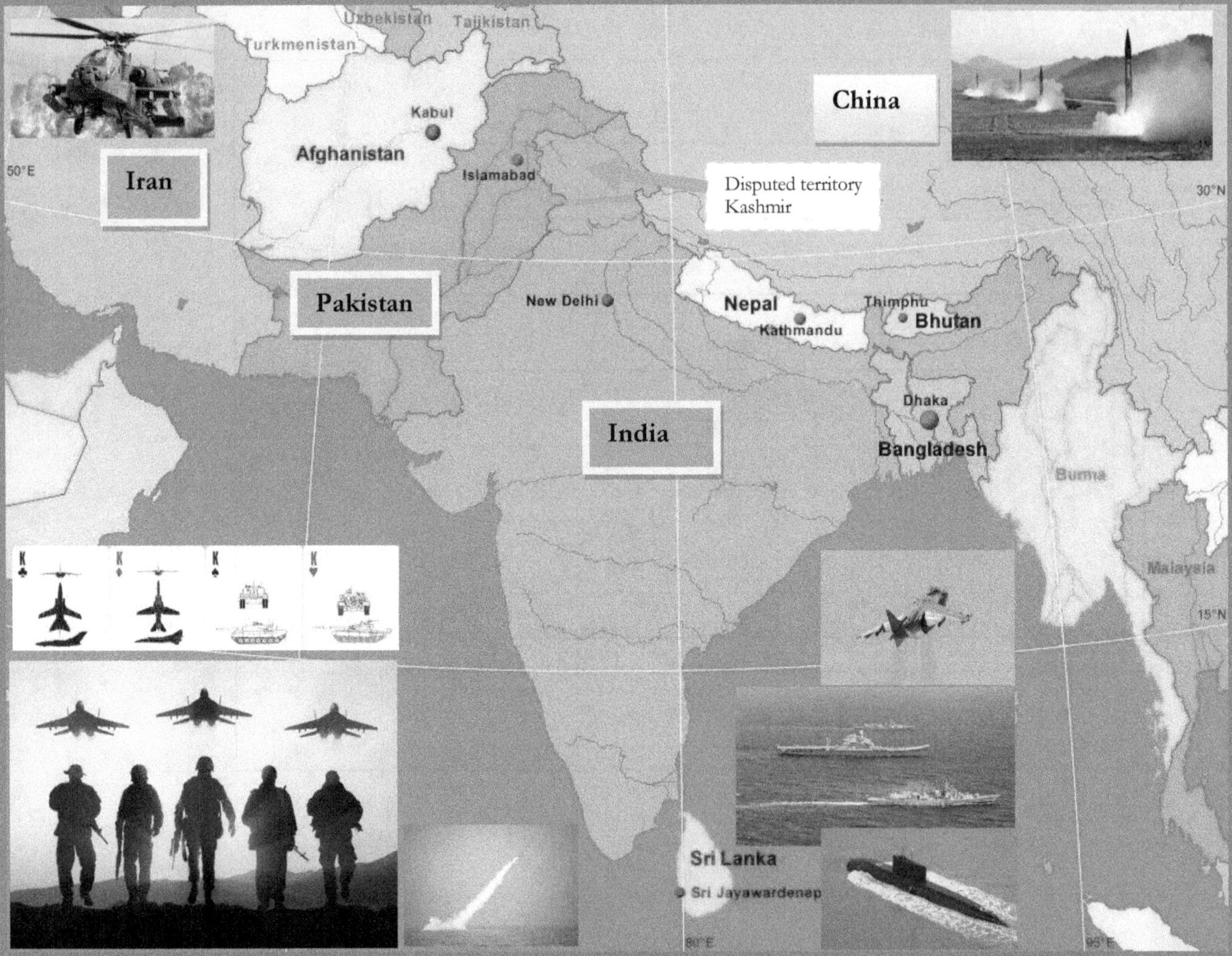

Countries Bordering Pakistan – (Afghanistan, China, India and Iran)

Al-Zarrar Pakistan Army MBT

Defence budgets in countries bordering Pakistan (2017)

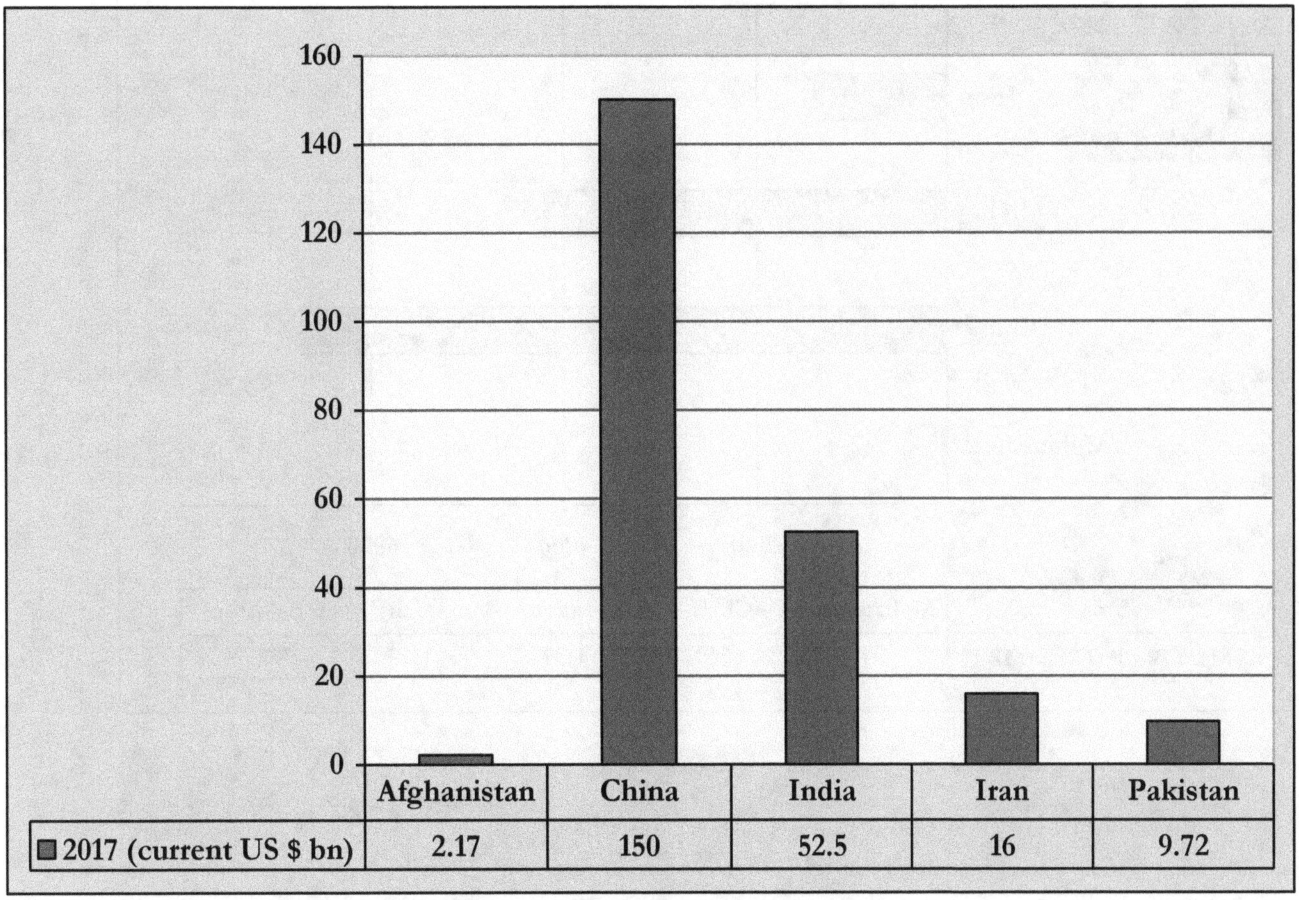

	Afghanistan	China	India	Iran	Pakistan
2017 (current US $ bn)	2.17	150	52.5	16	9.72

Defence budgets[162]

---

[162] Chapter six: Asia. (2017). *The Military Balance, 117*(1), 237-350.

Pakistan's neighbour's distribution of main battle tanks (MBT), 2017

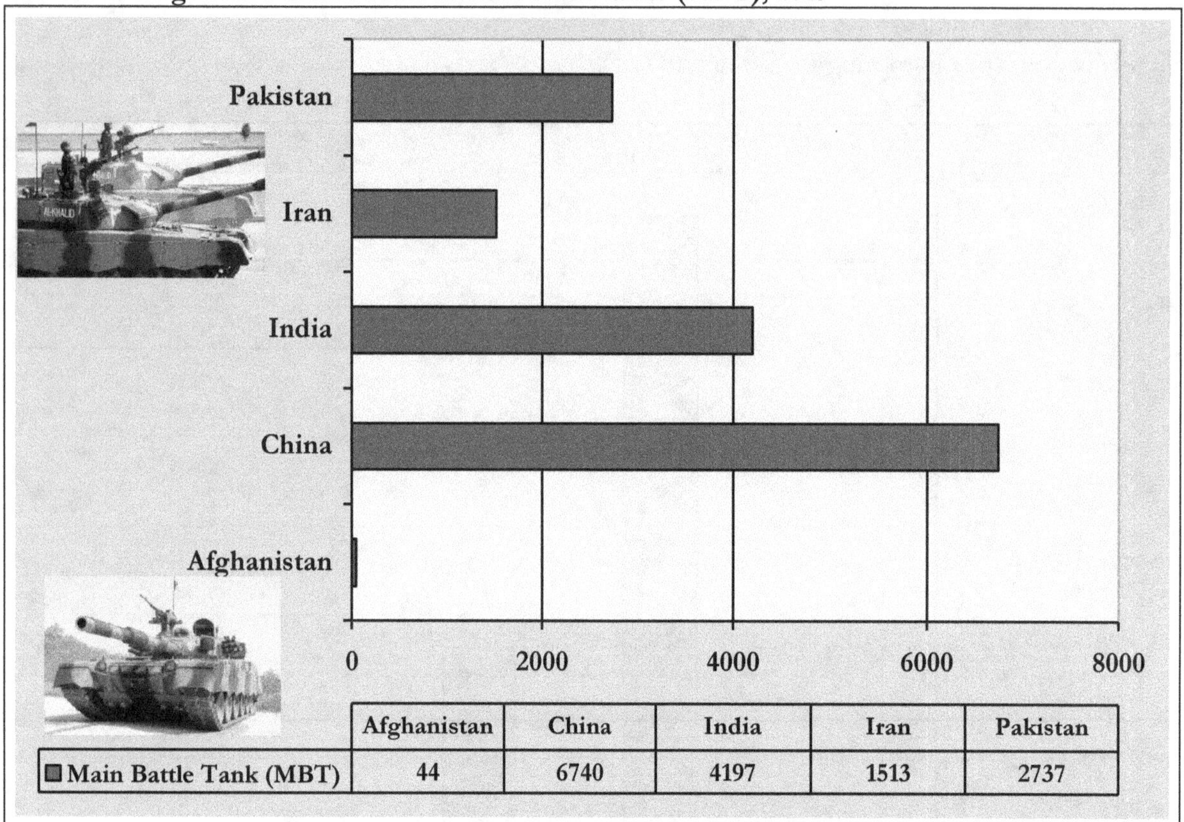

	Afghanistan	China	India	Iran	Pakistan
Main Battle Tank (MBT)	44	6740	4197	1513	2737

Indian Arjun Main Battle Tank

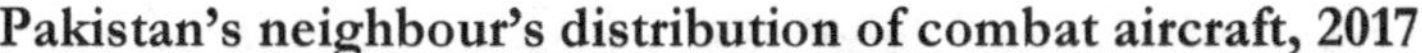

Pakistan's neighbour's distribution of combat aircraft, 2017

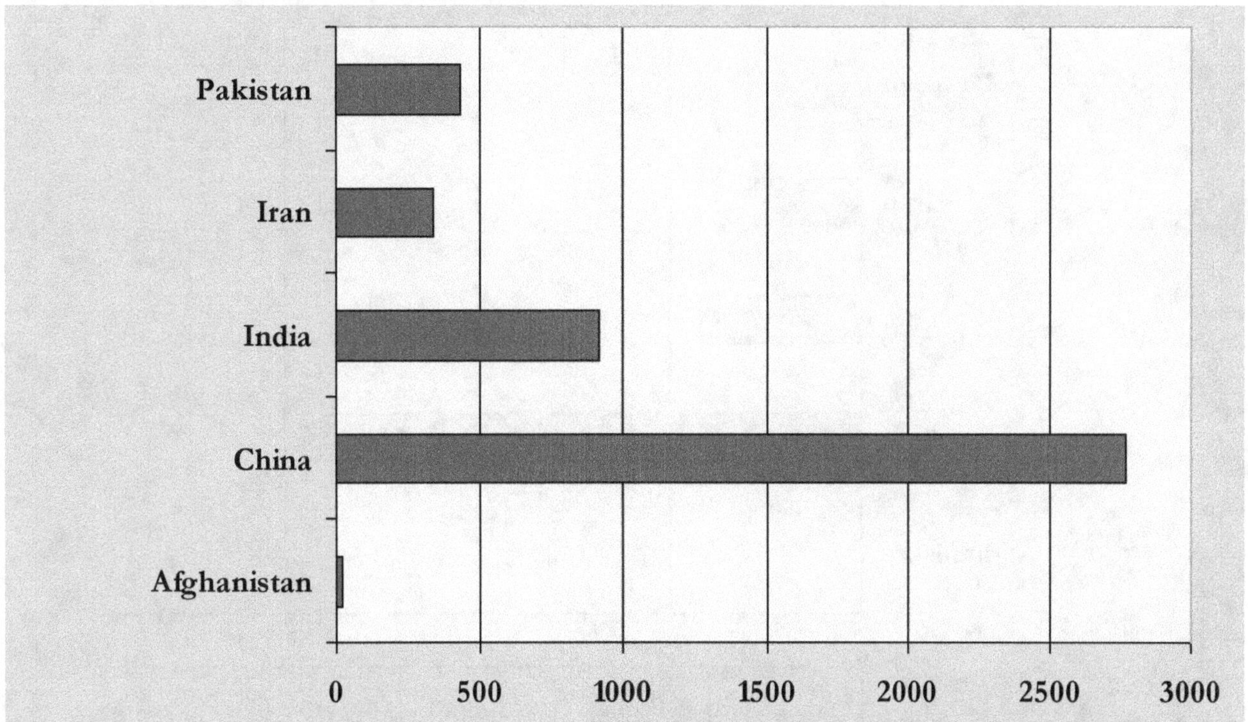

	Afghanistan	China	India	Iran	Pakistan
Combat Aircraft (2017)	19	2771	918	337	432

PAF F-16 Falcon releasing 2 smart munitions on to a given target

Pakistan's neighbour's distribution of principle surface warships and submarines, 2017

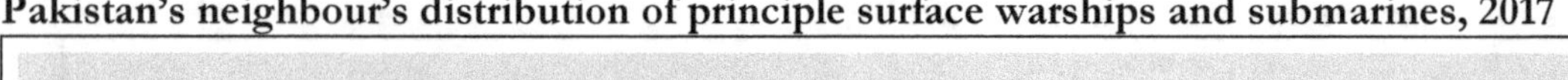

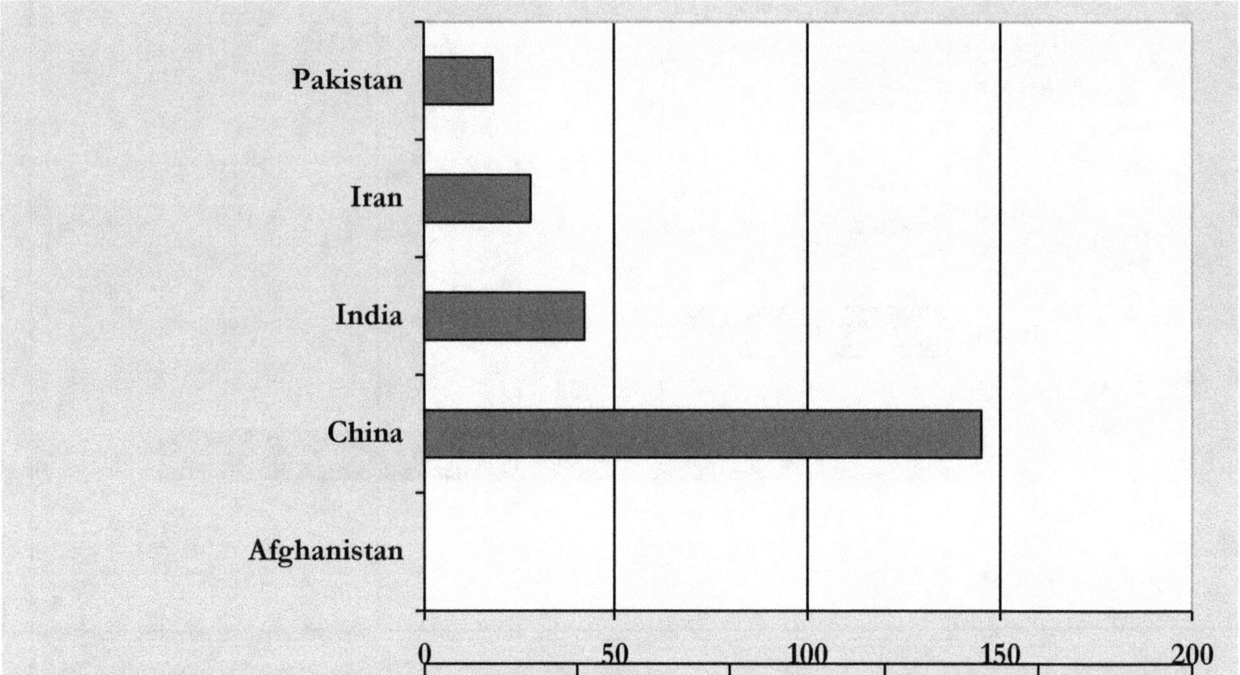

	Afghanistan	China	India	Iran	Pakistan
Principle surface warships and Submarines (2017)	0	145	42	28	18

A MiG-29K fighter takes off from the Indian Navy's new Vikramaditya aircraft carrier

Arms purchases

As they restructure their armed forces, the nations have become fervent consumers of military hardware produced in the United States, Russia, Britain, France, and other highly industrialized nations. The arms procured in these dealings are often the most sophisticated types obtainable, and they include the latest in fire-control radars, electronic warfare systems, and the like. In addition the wealthier nations of the region also have mounted a significant military-industrial effort by setting up home-based arms factories. Countries such as China, India, Iran and Pakistan have industries capable of building all main types of weapons, such as combat aircraft, helicopters, guided missiles, armoured vehicles, and surface ships.

The military arms build-up in the region has the essential components of an integrated, long-range strategic plan. The nations of this region are well on their way toward building a large and diversified military-industrial complex. As the nations in this region increase their defence expenditures and continue to import sophisticated weapons and at the same time expand their arms-making capabilities, their overall military capabilities will constantly improve, as will the threat they pose to their neighbours and rivals. This is the kind of settings in which regional arms races can speed up and spin out of control. [163]

Pakistani troops on a security patrol

---

[163] Klare, op cit:58

Image/pexels.com/F-16 Falcon silhouette

Military capabilities, 2018

Pakistan and its neighbour's military capacity

	Afghanistan	China	India	Iran	Pakistan
Population	34,124,811	1,387,096,243	1,281,935,911	82,021,564	204,924,861
GDP (2017) $bn	21.1 bn	11.9tr	2.44 tr	428 bn	279 bn (2016)
Defence budget $bn (2017)	2.17 bn	150bn	52.5bn	16.0 bn	9.72bn
Armed Forces Manpower	174,300	2,035,000	1,395,100	523,000	653,800

Reserves	unknown	510,000	1,155,000	350,000	500,000
Paramilitary	148,700	660,000	941,000	40,000	282,000
Main Battle Tank	44 (including 24 in store)	6,740 (723 LT TK)	4,197 (including 1,100 in store)	1,513+ (80 LT TK)	2,737 (including 270 in store)
AIFV/APC	996	8,880	2,836	1,250+	1,715
Artillery	775	13,258+	9,684+	6,798+	4,472+
Principal Surface warships	n/a	83	28	7 (Corvettes)	10
Submarines	n/a	62	14	21	8
Combat Aircraft	19	2,771	918	337	432
Armed Helicopters	4	246	19	50	42
Multi-role Helicopters	106	862	787	220+	216
Strategic Missiles (Nuclear)	0	475+	54+	40+	60+

Source: Based primarily on material in the IISS Military Balance 2017-2018, London, Routledge, 2018. Some data estimated or corrected by the author.

Range of Pakistan weapons

Pakistan Military Parade on 23rd March 2014 - Installed on the M113 armoured personnel carriers are the TOW-2 ATGMs

Chapter 7: Hybrid Wars and the Implications of this on Pakistan's Security

"War is not an independent phenomenon, but the continuation of politics by different means".

- Carl von Clausewitz

For Pakistan, it has been argued by many that the fourth generation/Hybrid war has been imposed in order to break the nation (Balkanization of Pakistan into different parts) with the aim of making it either extremely weak or total destruction as a nation state (so that it is not able to challenge their hegemonistic ambitions in this area).

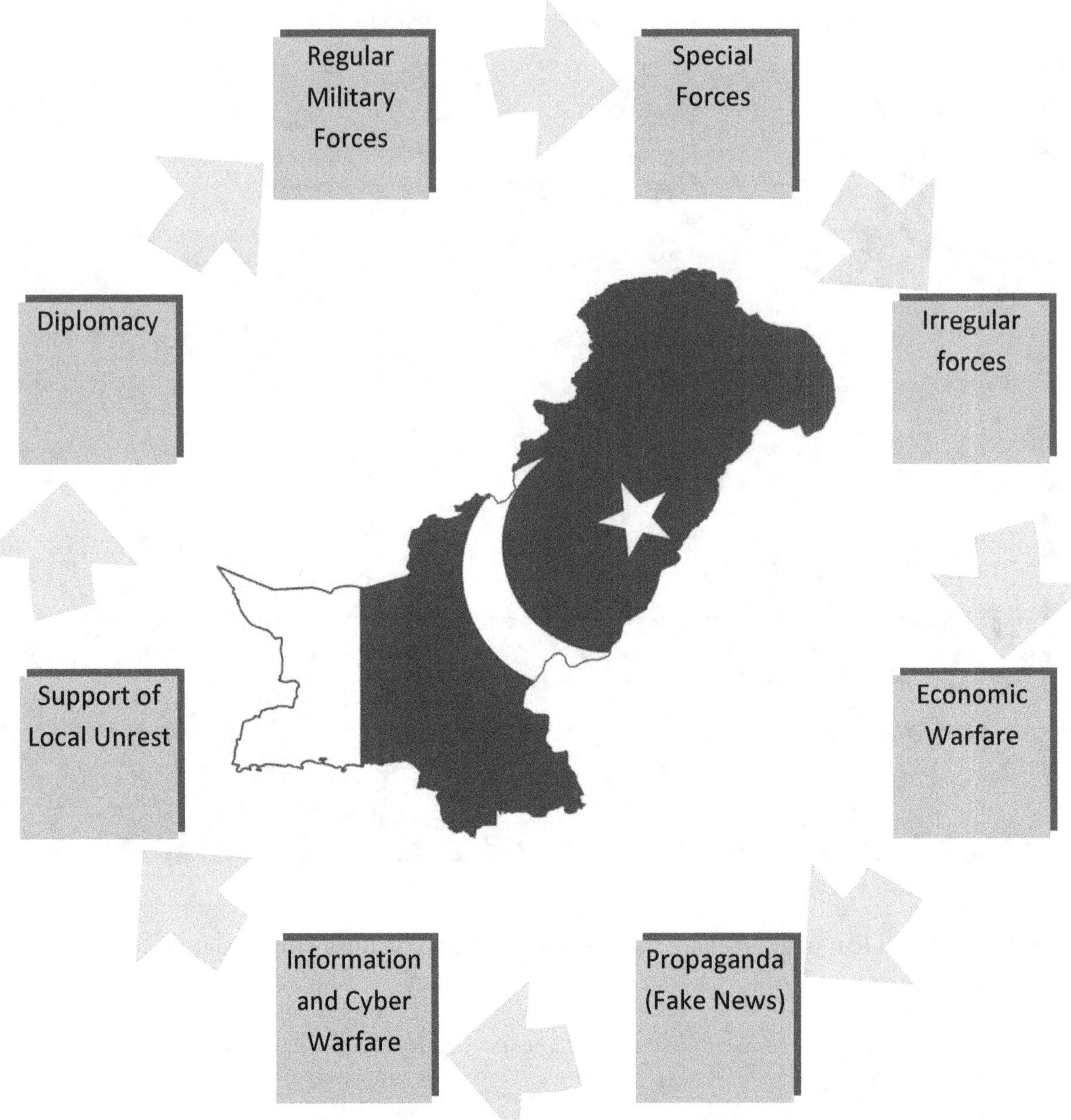

The Objectives of foreign powers are to destabilise Pakistan through a number of methods, such as its development projects. The aim is to weaken Pakistan's position on the international front and allow Indian hegemony in this part of the globe.

A number of tactics are being used by Pakistan's adversaries:

- Use of non-state actors

- Proxy wars (ethnic conflicts to be engineered)
- Encourage and Support local unrest
- Intensification of Propaganda war (Fake news/Psychological warfare)
- Target and undermine political leadership
- Use all opportunities to cripple the nation and put military and political pressure
- Attempt to undermine economy and project nation as a 'failed state'
- Attack the nations cohesivity and encourage divisions amongst its populations.
- Give public platform to extremist and terrorists in Pakistan (international propaganda of an independent separatist/terrorist movement such as the BLA)
- Multi-pronged attacks from all directions – Information and Cyber warfare, Attack on its culture, bogus human rights issues to be intensified, global political pressures by intense lobbying and blackmailing, encouraging residency to the US of corrupt and 'traitorous' people such as the former Pakistani ambassador to the USA, fund and increase criminality, terrorism, proxy wars, continue to encourage and support corrupt regimes/governments in Pakistan etc.
- Intense 'fake news' channels and websites to a negative global limelight and hence an excuse to undertake any international interventions in the future.
- Scapegoating Pakistan's for all the ills plaguing the US and its allies in the South Asian region.

A brief look at some of the tactics used against Pakistan:

The Ethnic conflicts

Encouraging and supporting ethnic conflicts In Pakistan. India with the support of its allies is encouraging and fomenting unrest in the aim of destabilising and weakening Pakistan. Terrorist such as the BLA, BLF have been given sophisticated arms to wage war on the Integrity of Pakistan. There are numerous evidence of proof that Indian RAW, with US CIA, Afghanistan KGB are supplying weapons to these terrorist groups, especially with development of the Gwadar port (a collaboration with China and Pakistan)/CPEC project that is viewed as a significant investment in Pakistan's development.

India's investment In Afghanistan is used as a pretext to undermine neighbouring Pakistan. It is giving an opportunity to destabilize Pakistan and create a major rift between the two Muslim countries. In addition, the funding of RAW to a political party in Pakistan (MQM) is a further proof of this attempt to cause instability.[164]

The Sectarian Divide

The Sunni-Shia rivalry has been exploited by a number of countries for their own vested interests. Pakistan has the largest number of Shia population after Iran. There have been many sectarian attacks in the country with the aim of initiating a sectarian conflict – divide and conquer scheme. Traditionally Saudi Arabia and Iran's competition for leadership of the Muslim world has resulted in these countries supporting and sponsoring havoc in Pakistan. The aim of increasing the sectarian divide has on the whole failed so far – due primarily to the strong military's dealing with this threat.

Pakistan's adversaries are using and exploiting any means to cause disharmony and internal conflict. Evidence of this has been found amongst a number of foreign intelligence agencies operations in Pakistan. The sectarian card will also benefit Iran who currently have strong ties with India's Hindu fundamentalist government of Prime minister Modi.

---

[164] Anam Sheikh (2017), India's hybrid warfare in Pakistan - https://www.globalvillagespace.com/indias-hybrid-warfare-in-pakistan/

Iran is allowing India to develop0 the Chabar sea port in direct competition to Pakistan's Gwadar project. Also tension on the Iranian and Pakistani borders have on occasions intensified with a number of fatalities on both sides. An Iranian spy drone was shot by the PAF in 2017.

International Isolation

There has been an attempt in isolating Pakistan on an international level, India has spearheaded in this direction and other countries such as the USA have also attempted to do this. For the USA, it is extremely upset and humiliated that the War in Afghanistan has cost them trillions of dollars and so far its longest serving war of 17 years with no result of 'winning' this war. Despite this duration, the USA with Afghan forces only occupy 40% of the territory, the remaining 60% is in the hands of the Taliban. The USA inability to defeat the Taliban have led them to scapegoat Pakistan for their own failings.

The only superpower with the most powerful military alliance (NATO) has not been able to defeat the Taiban and hence attribute this to the Pakistani's. The Pakistan government has recommended that a military victory is not achievable and that negotiations with the Taliban would be fruitful for all – however the American led 'ego' is unable to see this and is bent on 'teaching' Pakistan a lesson. It has attempted to put Pakistan on the terrorist sponsoring nations and with India is trying to undermine the integrity of the nation.

India has attempted to malign Pakistan's image, especially with the Hindu fundamentalist prime minister Modi wooing of foreign powers about Pakistan's alleged terrorism support. The Kashmir freedom struggle is being tarnished as a terrorist support, when in actually it has been a freedom struggle from Indian occupation. Intense Indian and Zionist lobbyists in Washington have started to cause major friction between Pakistan and USA. Indian Prime minister Modi and US President Trump declaring Sayeed Salahuddin as a terrorist was an attempt at weakening Pakistan's case on Kashmir. Negative view of Pakistan is predominantly given on Indian and Western Media – psychologically undermining Pakistan's credibility to the average person.[165]

The pseudo-liberals and Religious extremists

Pakistan also faces an insidious threat from the Pseudo-Liberals (some have been promoting Islamophobia) and religious extremists (with their own brand of wrong religious thought). These two groups have tried to eradicate the real Islamic Identity Of Pakistan – a Muslim Identity of mainstream Islam (the middle way, not too lose or too extreme). They have attempted to confuse and divide the nation – Pakistan has a number of ethnic groups and provinces, the only thing uniting them is their Islamic ideology. Pakistan's adversaries are trying their best to cause divisions within this area and have supported both sides to cause disharmony in the country – this would weaken Pakistan and its adversaries will an hedgemonistic control of this country. [166]

Political Standoff

Pakistan also faces aspects of a US inspired regime change to ensure a compliant political leadership, which has no commitments to Pakistan's self-interest. To do this, US foreign policy is to actively promote the political fragmentation and Balkanization of Pakistan as a state. Us desires a Pakistani leadership that will serve its global hegemonistic ambitions.[167] It intends to weaken the central government and cause divisions amongst the federal structure. The US has had access to various military bases in Pakistan and has used the 'war on terror' as the pretext for this – US Special Forces are expected to vastly expand their presence in Pakistan as part of training and counter-terrorism units.

---

[165] Anam Sheikh (2017), India's hybrid warfare in Pakistan - https://www.globalvillagespace.com/indias-hybrid-warfare-in-pakistan/

[166] Ibid.

[167] Prof Michel Chossudovsky (2012), The Destabilization of Pakistan - http://www.globalresearch.ca/images/harita_b.jpeg

The Balkanization of Pakistan

A Yugoslav-like fate was predicted by the US National Intelligence Council (NIC) and the US Central Intelligence Agency (CIA) in 2005. It was predicted that the country would in a civil war like scenario, inter-provisional rivalries and much bloodshed. Pakistan was deemed to become a 'failed state' with complete Talibanisation and lose its control of its nuclear weapons.[168] For Pakistan this was a sign that foreign powers were trying to 'engineer' this kind of scenario and were utilising all means of carrying out their plans of 'splitting Pakistan into different pieces – balkanization of Pakistan'.

Pakistan began to take appropriate measures to ensure that this foreign engineered plan did not materialise. Accordingly to the NIC and CIA scenario, "Pakistan will not recover easily from decades of political and economic mismanagement, divisive policies, lawlessness, corruption and ethnic friction,"[169] The US and its allies (including Israel and India) had planned to encourage social, ethnic and factional divisions with the aim of the territorial breakup of Pakistan. The US strategy was to redraw the borders Iraq, Iran, Syria, Turkey, Afghanistan and Pakistan. According to professor Michel Chossudovsky, **"This US agenda for Pakistan is similar to that applied throughout the broader Middle East Central Asian region. US strategy, supported by covert intelligence operations, consists in triggering ethnic and religious strife, abetting and financing secessionist movements while also weakening the institutions of the central government".[170]**

Pakistan's Oil and Gas reserves

Pakistan has extensive sources of oil, gas and untapped mineral resources, especially in its Baluchistan province. It has a number of projects that caused considerable interest from its adversaries – who do not want a strong economic and stable Pakistan. Economic prosperity will further enhance its defensive and offensive capability and would 'check mate' and potential threat from its enemies.

- Baluchistan province comprises over 40% of Pakistan's land mass
- Pakistan is thought to have an estimated 25.1 trillion cubic feet (Tcf) of proven gas reserves of which 19 trillion are located in Baluchistan.
- Pakistan had proven oil reserves of 300 million barrels (according to the Oil and Gas Journal) and other estimates are six trillion barrel of oil reserves - most of which are located in Baluchistan.
- Potential Iran-Pakistan pipeline corridor (also to include India if relationship improves) is poised to transit through Pakistan's Baluchistan province
- Gwadar deep sea port (financed by China) will give access to China and other countries of the supplies of Oil/Gas and other goods. This would improve the economic prospects for Pakistan and ensure a new trading route to a number of countries, including Central asia.

Covert Support to Baluchistan militants

Pakistan's Baluchistan province has seen evidence of foreign sponsored aid to militants who are trying to separate or breakaway from Pakistan. The militant leaders have been given refuge in India and western countries and indicate the levels of support from these areas. There is evidence that the US and its allies (CIS, KHAD,RAW etc.) are trying to woo and foment troubles in this region. Sophisticated arms are being provided to these misguided militants (a tiny segment of these militants are causing problems).

---

[168] Prof Michel Chossudovsky (2012), The Destabilization of Pakistan - http://www.globalresearch.ca/images/harita_b.jpeg
[169] Ibid,
[170] Ibid.

Professor Michel Chossudovsky says, **"The stated purpose of US counter-terrorism is to provide covert support as well as as training to "Liberation Armies" ultimately with a view to destabilizing sovereign governments. In Kosovo, the training of the Kosovo Liberation Army (KLA) in the 1990s had been entrusted to a private mercenary company, Military Professional Resources Inc (MPRI), on contract to the Pentagon. The BLA bears a canny resemblance to Kosovo's KLA, which was financed by the drug trade and supported by the CIA and Germany's Bundes Nachrichten Dienst (BND)"**.

Baloch population in Pink: In Iran, Pakistan and Southern Afghanistan

There is evidence that foreign countries including the USA are favouring the dismemberment of Pakistan's Baluchistan province into a 'greater Baluchistan, which would also incorporate the Sistan province in Iran'. This would to territorial loss for Pakistan and Iran. The war on terror is helping the US and its allies engineer a breakup of Pakistan – It is also making it difficult for it to get favourable international loans it needs to help it stabilise economically. The US has influenced IMF and other global financial institutions of putting more indirect pressure that could cause the central government to collapse, thereby not having the ability to allocate resources to the federal governments. The potential is for the federal governments to be unhappy and more chances of it being influenced by external agencies to break away and ensure the loss of Pakistan's territorial integrity.

There have attempts by the US to study on ways of splitting Pakistan up – a study undertaken by US Lieutenant Colonel Ralph Peters in 2006 (writing for 'The Armed Forces Journal') showed this and became further evidence of the US's thought process in engineering the dismemberment of Pakistan. Pakistan should be broken up, leading to the formation of a separate country - Greater Baluchistan or Free Balochistan (incorporating the Pakistani and Iranian Baloch provinces into a single political entity).

Furthermore, Pakistan's North West Frontier Province (NWFP)/Khyber Punktunwa should be incorporated into Afghanistan "because of its linguistic and ethnic affinity". This proposed fragmentation would reduce Pakistani territory to approximately 50 percent of its present land area and also loose a large part of its coastline on the Arabian Sea.. Even though the map does not officially reflect the US Pentagon's doctrine, it is thought to have been used in many training programs for senior military officers.[171]

---

[171] Prof Michel Chossudovsky (2012), The Destabilization of Pakistan - http://www.globalresearch.ca/images/harita_b.jpeg

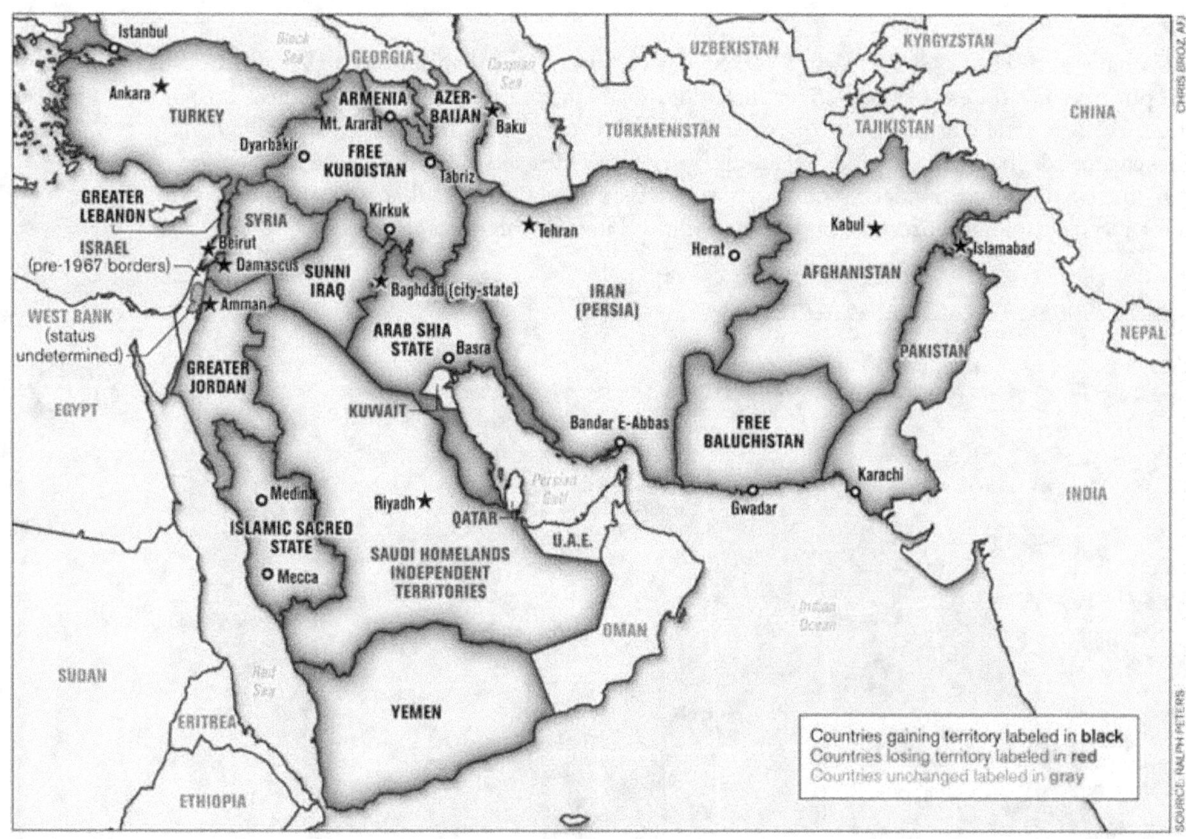

Other influential papers are also calling for the Balkanization of Pakistan, the Huffington Post with the sub-heading of 'breaking Pakistan to Fix it', states the following, **"The argument for Balkanizing Pakistan or, more specifically, fragmenting the Islamic Republic so it's easier to police and economically develop, has been on the table since Pakistan's birth in 1947…. And lately, the concept is looking more appealing by the day, because as a result of flawed boundaries combined with the nexus between military rule and Islamic extremism, Pakistan now finds itself on a rapid descent toward certain collapse and the country's leaders stubbornly refuse to do the things required to change course. But before allowing Pakistan to commit state suicide, self-disintegrate and further destabilize the region, the international community can beat them to the punch and deconstruct the country less violently"**.[172]

In 2012 an American congressman, Dana Rohrabacher (Republican of California) proposed a bill that called for the secession of Pakistan's largest province, Baluchistan. Dana Rohrabacher, stated that the people of Baluchistan, a sprawling western province racked by a seven-year-old separatist insurgency, should "have the right to self-determination and to their own sovereign country." This resulted in a furious response from Pakistani politicians and media, with Prime Minister Yousaf Raza Gilani calling it an attack on Pakistani sovereignty.[173]

---

[172] Michael Hughes, Balkanizing Pakistan: A Collective National Security Strategy - https://www.huffingtonpost.com/michael-hughes/balkanizing-pakistan-a-co_b_635950.html

[173] New York Times (2012) Fury in Pakistan after US congressman suggests that a province leaves
http://www.nytimes.com/2012/02/22/world/asia/fury-in-pakistan-after-us-congressman-suggests-that-aprovince-leave.html

The Pakistani's have accused Mr. Rohrabacher of seeking to "balkanize" Pakistan and that the USA is attempting to put pressure on establishing covert listening posts on the border with Iran. The Pakistanis feel that the senator was acting at the behest of American intelligence agents. In 2011 a border incident in which US helicopters deliberately targeted 2 Pakistani posts in which led to 24 Pakistani Soldiers being killed, though the US disputed on details of the border clash. For Pakistan, this was another way of putting military and psychological pressure on Pakistan if it did not comply with US desires.[174]

Maps Redrawn - Pakistan Fears for the Worst

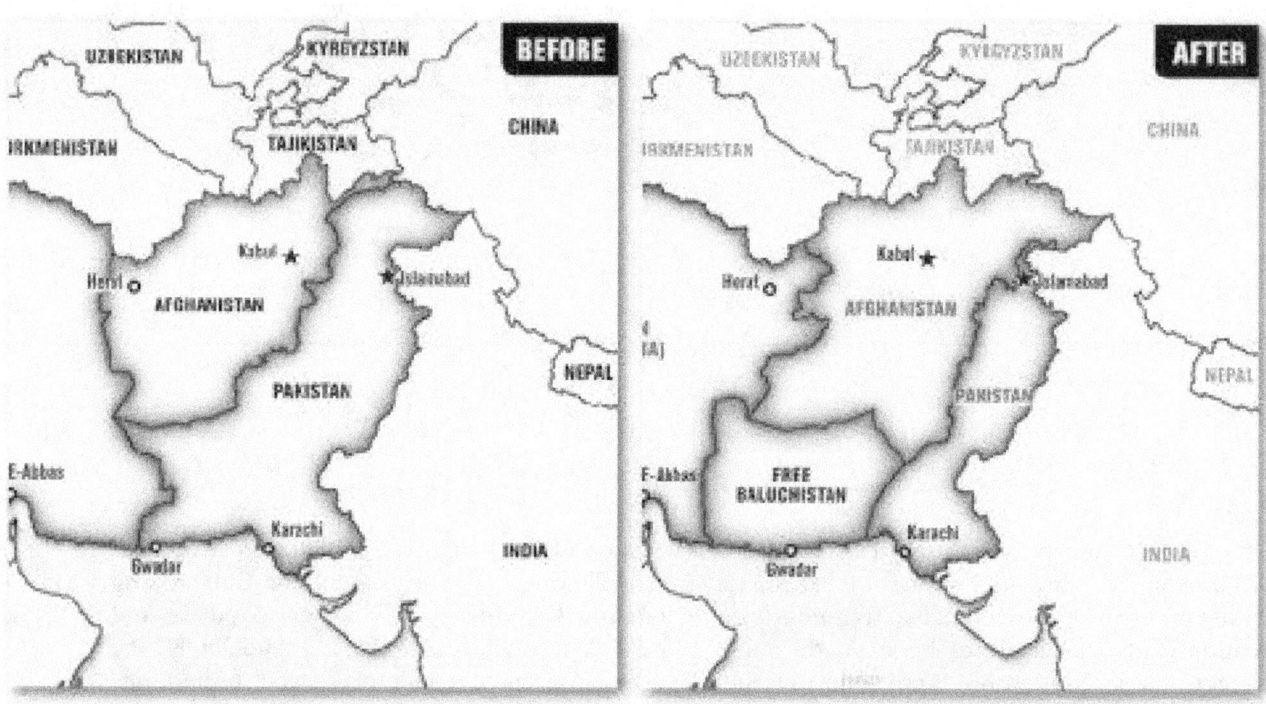

A Controversial Imagining of Borders Above are sections of maps that originally accompanied a speculative June 2006 article by Ralph Peters in Armed Forces Journal that has concerned Pakistanis.

The above map and the various statements from US congressman and the negative media propaganda against it (primarily in India and the Western World) has led to Pakistan feeling betrayed by the US and has fueled a belief that that the United States really wants to breakup Pakistan. Pakistan fears, that the US in collaboration with Afghanistan, India and covert Zionist support from Israel are attempting to destroy Pakistan. The recent US tilt towards India has further corroborated these beliefs.[175]

Brigadier Asif Haroon Raja, states the following, **" The US ignores its own human rights violations and also looks the other way to massive human rights abuses committed by Israel, India, Egypt and other dictatorial regimes towing its agenda. Washington, however, has no tolerance for democratic regimes that refuse to**

---

[174] New York Times (2012) Fury in Pakistan after US congressman suggests that a province leaves
http://www.nytimes.com/2012/02/22/world/asia/fury-in-pakistan-after-us-congressman-suggests-that-aprovince-leave.html

[175] New York Times, Maps Redrawn , Pakistan Fears for the Worst - https://mt360.wordpress.com/2008/11/24/maps-redrawn-pakistan-fears-the-worst/

make their countries compliant States and opt to pursue independent foreign policy best suited for their national interests. Various excuses are manufactured to bring suchlike defiant States in line. The more often dirty tactics in use are sanctions, orchestrated political turmoil and chaos, coercion, threats, proxy war, psychological operations, propaganda, regime change, and if needed, physical assault and occupation of targeted country".[176]

He further states, " The Indo-US-Israel nexus is adept in contriving a false narrative to build a case against a country. Going by the dictum of Joseph Goebbels, the trio repeatedly utter lies and half-truths to convert falsehood into truth and convincing the audience to accept black as white. The targeted ruling regime is demonized and discredited under a well-planned media campaign to justify intervention and a regime change".[177]

Brigadier Asif Haroon Raja, further highlights the US and its allies tactics in the region, "Since 9/11, the US has used proxies, terrorism, sedition, propaganda war and coercive tactics as tools to destabilize the targeted country. It has meddled in internal affairs of Afghanistan, Iraq, Syria, Libya, Tunisia, Egypt, Sudan, Somalia, Chad, Turkey, Iran and Pakistan. All are Islamic countries and their peoples are all Muslims".[178]

Historically Pakistan has a long time ally relationship with the US, but at critical times it was let down. The US under the influence of strong zionist lobbies in the USA have drastically focused primarily on the Muslim world and have gradually caused divisions and destructions of the countries in the region – one by one it is attempting to weaken and destroy all countries that have the potential to be strong and assertive.

Accordingly, Brigadier Asif Haroon Raja states, "The second Afghan war that immediately followed the 9/11 brought back Pakistan in the good books of the US and it was quickly made a non-NATO ally. This was, however, a deception since Pakistan was in reality a target and was to be destabilized, denuclearized and Balkanized covertly. After brewing up war on terror in FATA, Khyber Pakhtunkhwa and Baluchistan, Pakistan was subjected to cooked-up allegations that it was in cahoots with the militants and that its nukes were unsafe. The hidden objective of the US was exposed in 2006 after the publication of an article in US Defence Journal titled "Blood Borders" written by Lt Col Ralph Peters. The map showed changed boundaries of Middle East, and Baluchistan a separate state".[179]

Furthermore, he argues, "The 'Do More' mantra introduced in 2005/06 was meant to brew political stabilization, bleed economy and foment insecurity. Indo-US-Israel-Western media campaign demonized Pakistan that it's Army and ISI were supporting terrorism. Idea was to discredit the Army, brand Pakistan a terror abetting State and Pak Army/ISI rogue outfits. A narrative was built that Pakistan was collapsing, nuclear arsenal was unsafe and its nukes might fall into wrong hands (Islamic extremists). Objective was to give an excuse to USA to declare Pakistan a failed State and to occupy Islamabad and the provinces of Punjab, Sindh and Baluchistan and seize nuclear arsenal".[180]

For Pakistan there has been a number of schemes for the country to be destablised. A senior Indian Navy officer Commander Kulbushan Yadhav was caught in Pakistan's Baluchistan province. He was travelling under the false name of Mubarak Hussain Patel and had been operating since 2003 at the Iranian Chahbahar port. He was given substantial money by India's RAW intelligence agency (allegedly upto $400 million) to plan and carryout a number of destablising and terrorist attacks in Pakistan. He and his handlers/workers were supplying weapons to the Baluchi terrorists (BLA etc.), gaining knowledge of Pakistan's Makran-Karachi seacoast for future amphibious landings,

---

[176] Brigadier Asif Haroon Raja, Pakistan Tribune (2018) USA's treacherous agenda against Pakistan - http://paktribune.com/articles/USAs-treacherous-agenda-against-Pakistan-243339.html

[177] Ibid.
[178] Ibid.
[179] Ibid.
[180] Brigadier Asif Haroon Raja, Pakistan Tribune (2018) USA's treacherous agenda against Pakistan - http://paktribune.com/articles/USAs-treacherous-agenda-against-Pakistan-243339.html

evidence of supplying money to the MQM mohajir party in Pakistan's Sind province, scare the chinese from investing in Gwadar sea port, Scuttle CPEC development. The USA was also thought to be supplyimng arms and attempting to antogonise the Pakistani population bordering afghanistan by contnuosly doing drone strikes so that they rebel against the central government (via CIA and Blackwater). The aim was to cause divisions between the civilian and military populations. It is alleged that NATO containers were also used for supplying arms.[181]

Pakistan is one of few countries that its population see as the only institution that is not corrupt like its Civilian counterparts. It has high esteem for its armed forces, and hence the aim was to dilute and cause friction between the support of the people for its armed forces. The US had spent considerable amount of money in its operations in Baluchistan, according to Christina Fair (an American academic that has fervour of hatred against Pakistan and this is seen by many being on the payroll of foreign agencies) thye US had pumped in more money in Baluchistan than in Iran and yet has failed to make it independent.[182]

Pakistan has established even closer strategic relationship to its ally China and is making mends its realtionship with Russia. It is seeing the threats of destablisation and eventual balkanization of Pakistan's territorial integrity by 3 'axis of evil' – USA, India, Israel (zionist lobbies and indo-Israeli nexus) and a puppet Afghanistan government. All of these 'axis of evil' are influencing the US administraion and its allies to attack and strike Pakistan. It is looking for more excuses and is continually asking Pakistan to 'do more' mantra – Pakistan has started to reject these allegations and plans and has asked the USA to do more in its conflict on War on terror in Afghanistan.

Brigadier Asif Haroon Raja further states, **"Since August 22, 2017, he and senior US leaders have adopted a highly belligerent posture against Pakistan. Series of threatening statements have been issued and Pakistan put on notice. Pakistan's response that it has done enough and will not do any more, and that it is now the turn of USA and Afghanistan to do more is rational and logical. It has rightly rejected the US paltry aid, stressing it needs respect and acknowledgement of its sacrifices, and adding that it can keep fighting terrorism at its own without American assistance. Pakistan has discontinued military cooperation and intelligence sharing with USA, and has other effective options to exercise in case the US opts for a unilateral punitive action. Pakistan's principled stance seem to have mellowed down the jingoism of hawks in USA and they have started giving reconciliatory feelers".[183]**

The above are considered to be 4th generation wars, evolving to Hybrid wars on Pakistan. Many analysts have mentioned the threats that Pakistan is facing internally and externally. The folowing manp indicates the growing pressures that Pakistan has been put in.

---

[181] Ibid.

[182] Ibid.

[183] Ibid.

Hybrid Warfare on Pakistan

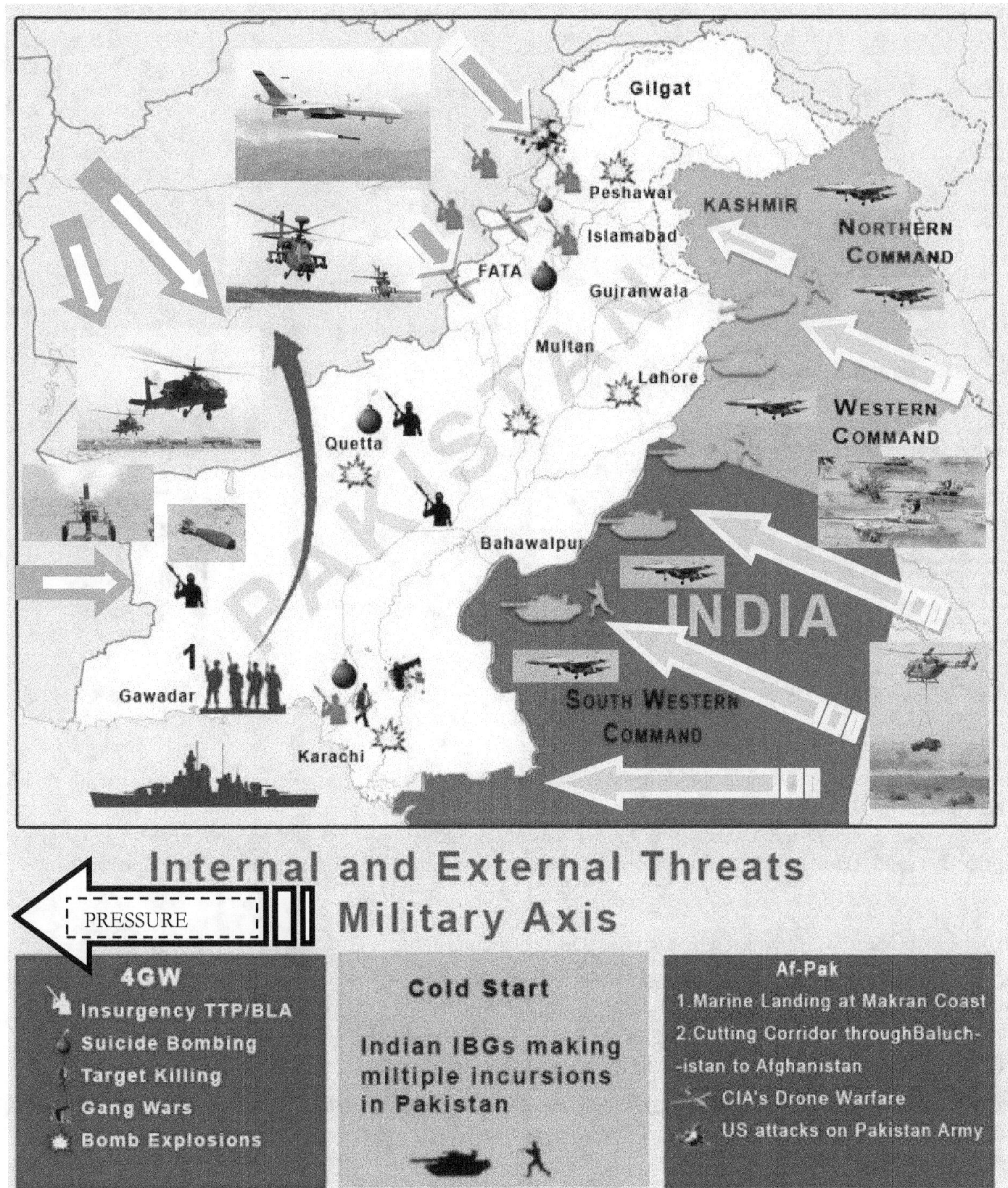

4G Warfare, Cold Start, Af-Pak deployed against Pakistan (modified map)[184]

---

[184] 4G Warfare, Cold Start, Af-Pak deployed against Pakistan - http://www.brasstacks.pk/ https://forum.bodybuilding.com/attachment.php?attachmentid=5204213&d=1356182812

The phrase '**axis of evil**' is used against countries that are accused of sponsoring terrorism, seeking weapons mass destruction, causing instability and planning to do serious harm to a nations territorial integrity. The Phrase was initially coined by U.S. President George W. Bush in his State of the Union address on January 29, 2002. Currently Pakistan has the following 'axis of evil' countries that are trying their best to weaken and dismember Pakistan.

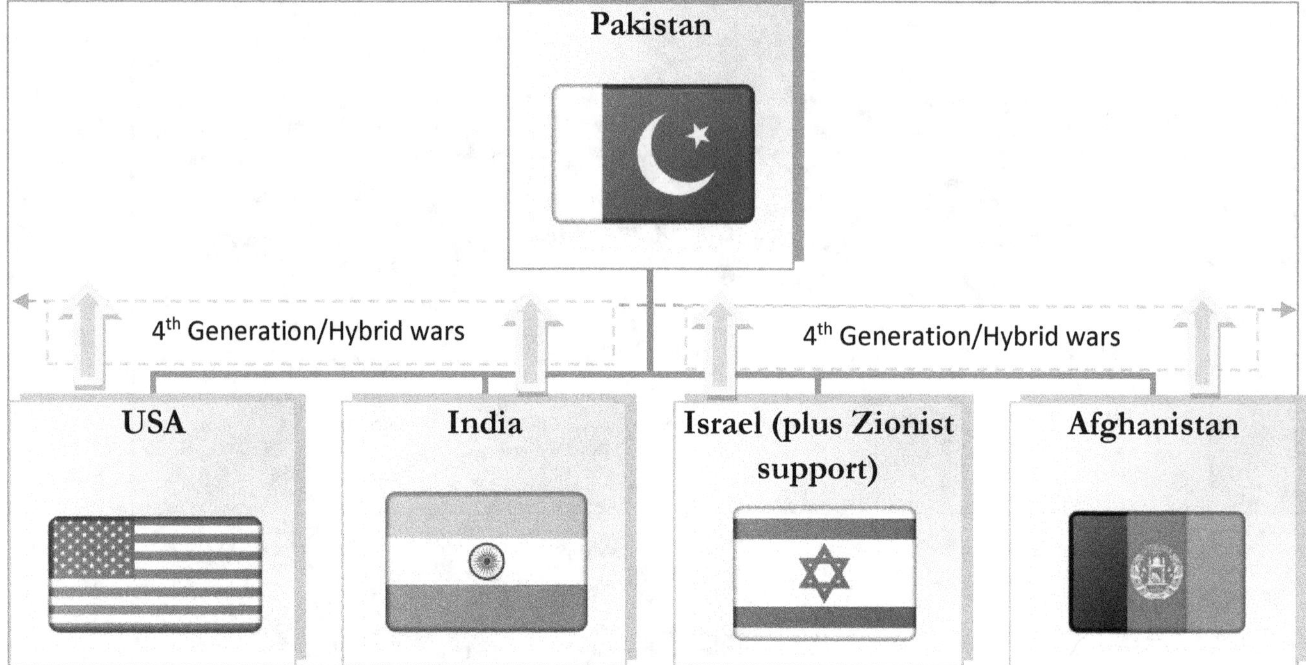

Pakistan's current 'Axis of Evil'

Pakistan has so far successfully thwarted the designs of its adversaries, but still has serious threats to deal with on all fronts. It has successfully carried out a number of operations to eradicate internal terrorist threats and to reduce external influences. The Director General of Inter Services Public Relations (ISPR) Major General Asif Ghafoor announced that Pakistan Army has successfully completed Operation Khyber-4. [185]The results of the operations were as follows:

- Scores of landmines were defused by the troops in the operation.
- Operation Khyber-4 was carried out with strong and complete planning - Every single terrorist in Rajgal and Shawal was targeted.
- Clearance operation had taken place in Khyber Valley, where 91 security checkposts have been set up.
- The military had consultation with NATO forces during the operation.
- Security forces have carried out 3300 operations under Radd-ul-Fasaad so far. In addition, Pakistan's 'Rangers had carried out 1728 operations across its Punjab province.

---

[185] Samaa.tv (2017) Pakistan Army successfully completes Operation Khyber-4 -
https://www.samaa.tv/pakistan/2017/08/pakistan-army-successfully-completes-operation-khyber-4/

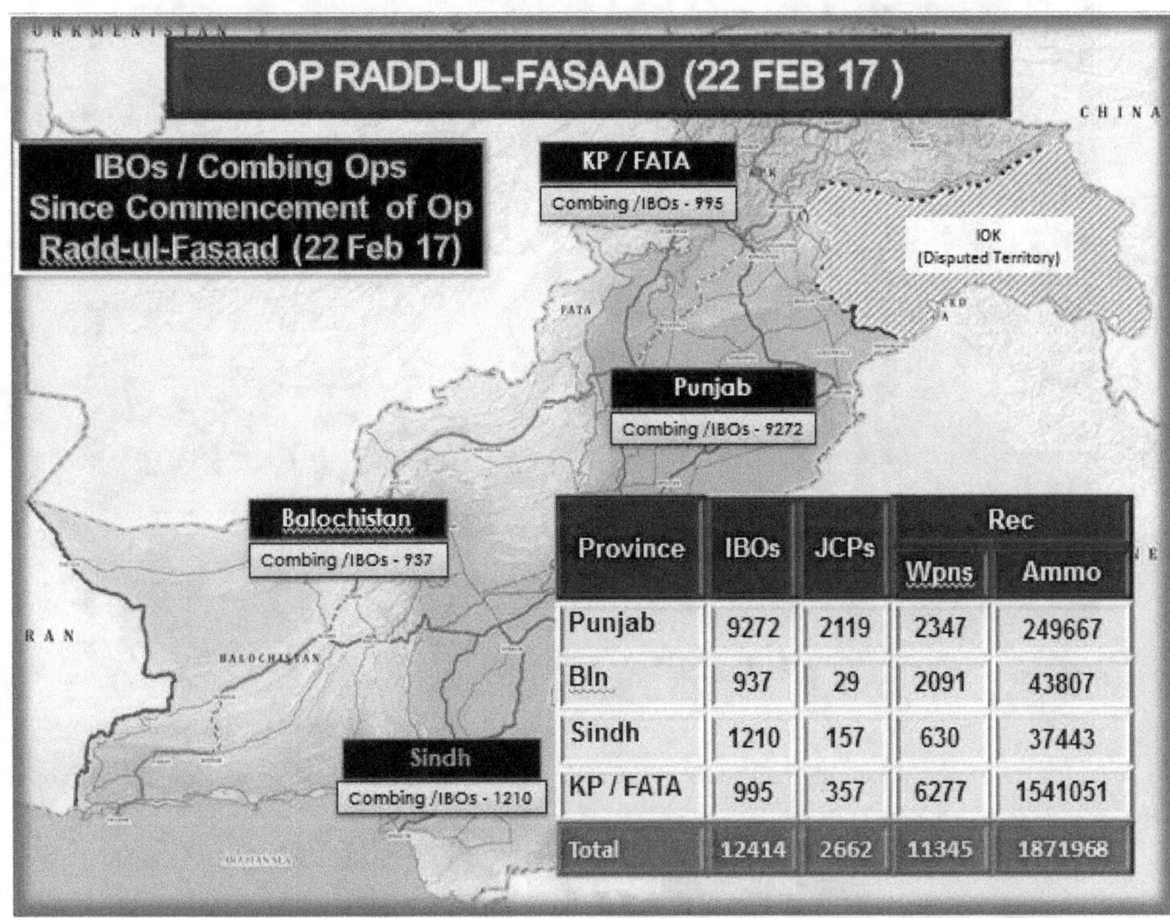

Province	IBOs	JCPs	Rec	
			Wpns	Ammo
Punjab	9272	2119	2347	249667
Bln	937	29	2091	43807
Sindh	1210	157	630	37443
KP / FATA	995	357	6277	1541051
Total	12414	2662	11345	1871968

Criminal activities have been drastically reduced in Pakistan's largest City Karachi as part of the security operations carried out.

CATEGORY	YEAR					
	2013	2014	2015	2016	2017	Total
IMPROVEMENT IN LAW & ORDER SITUATION						
Terrorist Incidents	57	66	18	16	1	158
Target Killing	965	602	199	89	34	1889
Extortion Cases	1524	899	303	101	56	2883
Kidnapping Cases	174	115	37	26	8	360

CATEGORY	YEAR					TOTAL
	2013	2014	2015	2016	2017	
Operations	1298	3086	2466	2022	1467	10339
Handed over to Police	1264	2358	2181	1207	1220	8230
Weapons	1917	3946	2819	1887	911	11480
Ammunition	101402	125552	196061	197811	112740	733356
Terrorist Apprehended	51	478	614	356	247	1746
Target Killer Apprehended	212	214	190	453	359	1428
Bhatta Collectors Apprehended	167	97	99	77	107	547
Kidnappers for Ransom Apprehended	14	27	49	28	18	136
Abductees Release from Kidnappers	10	25	103	13	2	153
RANGERS SACRIFICES						
Soldiers Shaheed	3	13	08	-		24
Soldiers Injured	17	37	23	5	12	94

In addition, 95 percent of displaced persons have also returned home with the Pakistan Army helping out.

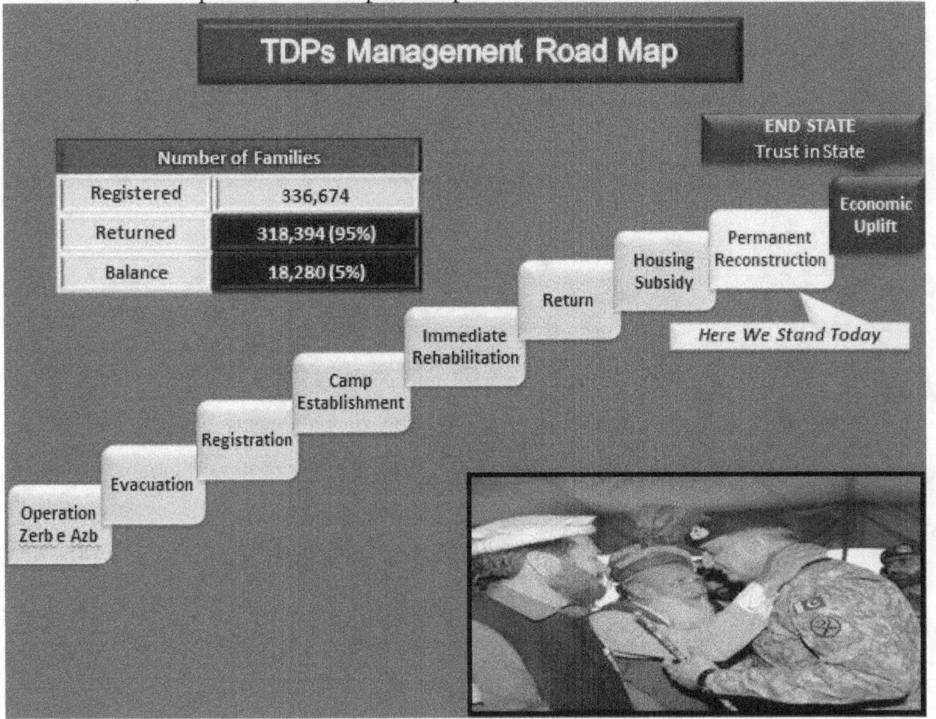

Border movements in Khyber Pakhtunkhwa have been made more effective – these have reduced the number of cross border attacks.

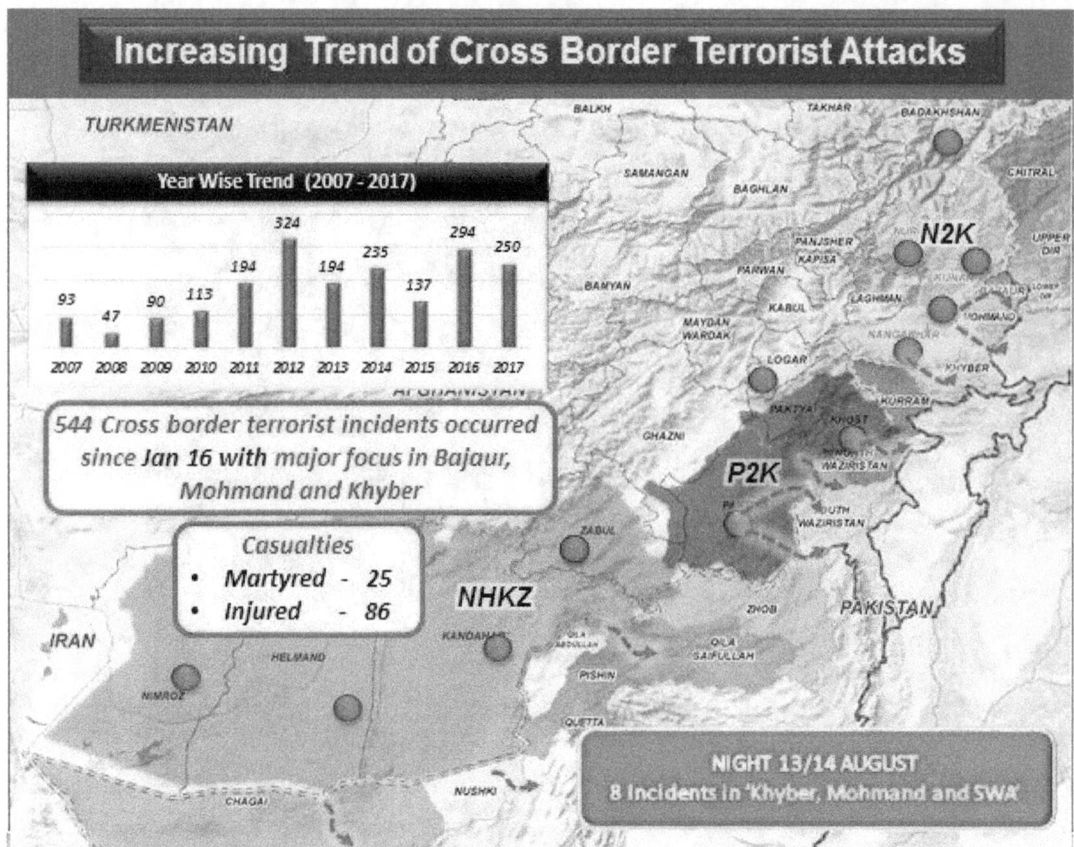

Pakistan has attempted to reduce terrorist activities that have been well planned and orchestrated by its adversaries. This has foiled the schemes against it but further pressure has been directly or indirectly applied to Pakistan.[186]

Pakistan's firepower in exercise Azm-e-Nau

---

[186] Samaa.tv (2017) Pakistan Army successfully completes Operation Khyber-4 - https://www.samaa.tv/pakistan/2017/08/pakistan-army-successfully-completes-operation-khyber-4/

Pakistan's firepower in exercise Azm-e-Nau

Pakistan Army aviation 'Cobra' gunship helicopter

Pakistani MBT on exercise Azm-e-Nau

Pakistan's army Nasr battlefield short range nuclear capable missile

<u>CONCLUSION</u>

Pakistan's main threat perceptions emanate from India. Its main concerns include India's military build-up, both conventionally and nuclear, and its ability to deliver nuclear payloads due to its ever-increasing ballistic capabilities (including the Prithvi and Agni surface-to-surface missiles and nuclear capable IAF fighters). India now has the nuclear command-and-control centres required to integrate nuclear weapons and related assets. Its Akash anti-missile missile, claimed to be superior to the US Patriot, is also being positioned to intercept incoming Ghauri and Hatf missiles, which has created another security headache for Pakistan's defence planners.[187]

India's assertive posture since the 1971 war has increased in the last few years, particularly following the advent of the BJP fundamentalist government. Although the BJP government has attempted to explain that India's military build-up is defensive and commensurate with India's overall economic growth, others in the region cannot be so sure of India's intentions.[188]

The area of concern for Western security analysts is the absence of proper command and control over the sub-continent nuclear arms race. Without the appropriate checks and balances, the 1.35 billion people of South Asia are vulnerable to a potential nuclear war between India and Pakistan. This grim prospect is enhanced given the intensity of distrust and active hostility over Kashmir. Any cross-border nuclear attack will arrive without sufficient warning for both sides, as the flight time of Prithvi or Ghauri missiles will be under three minutes, giving insufficient time for evacuation contingency or retaliatory response. The prospect of an unstable regime getting into power is also very

---

[187] News International, Armed to the Teeth, Jang Publishers Ltd, 1998, Pg10
[188] Johann Mcgeary, India's Surprise Nuclear Tests, The Time, May 25, 1998, Pg34

high on both sides. The ethnic unrest that is characteristic of the Indian sub-continent also highlights the dangers of a terrorist or dictatorial regime having access to weapons of mass destruction.[189]

Furthermore, the hostility of South Asian countries has contributed to the massive arms build-up in the region. The threat perceptions in this region has led these countries to purchase 'state-of-the-heart' sophisticated arms, this has resulted in altering the security of each country in the region. There is an urgent need that better sense prevails in New Delhi and nuclear militarisation is stopped. Pakistan's defence policy is basically reactive to Delhi's defence agenda. Nonetheless, there is an urgent need for confidence building measures to be positively integrated into both nations' foreign policies to ease tensions, and also for a focus on the real issues of poverty and illiteracy, instead of concentrating on tit-for-tat responses to each nation's rhetoric (see chapter 8).

Pakistan's other security concerns come from its western borders with Afghanistan and Iran. In the past, the Taliban control over most of Afghanistan and the killings of Iranian diplomats has strained the relations between the three neighbours. Tensions have risen between Iran and Afghanistan since, with Iran using the incidents as an excuse to conduct a 'military exercise' on its border with Afghanistan (mobilising over 200,000 troops and entering Afghan airspace),[190] in an exercise designed to warn the Taliban of Iran's unease with the new Afghan regime. This tension also led to much 'sabre rattling' between Iran and Pakistan, with the threat of conflict only subsiding after intense negotiations between the respective countries. In current times, the numerous small armes border incidents between Iran and Pakistan has increased tensions. The PAF had shot down an Iranian drone that was spying deep in Pakistan's Baluchistan province shows the mistrust with these two countries. This mistrust has increased due to the very close ties between India and Iran.

Pakistan is also concerned about potential threats emanating from other regions, such as Israel. The reported joint Indo-Israeli pre-emptive strike intended to destroy its nuclear facilities and the frequent reports of air incursion by Israeli and Indian aircraft, have only served to highlight Pakistani fears. There is also much more concern over the exporting of sophisticated Israeli military hardware and the close collaboration in nuclear ties between these two countries.[191] America's decision to impose punitive sanctions against Pakistan over its nuclear programme has also aggrieved the Pakistan government, which argues that it had no feasible option but to test, given the insufficient promises of aid from some western governments, after India revived its nuclear programme. Pakistan was unwilling to ditch its nuclear programme, after weighing up the options, as the inducement to not test was not sufficient to safeguard its security. In the past, the cruise missile attacks against Osama Bin Laden in Afghanistan also crossed Pakistan air space, further deteriorating the relationship with America.[192] The US war on terror has further destabilising the region and Pakistan is feeling the 'heat' from a so called ally that is seen to be ditching Pakistan and wooing India – allegedly to contain a rising China. The deliberate attack on Pakistani border post in which a number of Pakistani soldiers were killed, showed how quickly things can change.

Pakistan is also faced with multi-faceted threats from its immediate neighbours, India, Afghanistan, Iran, USA and also a potential Israel threat. Further compounding Pakistan's security fears is its internal problems, such as the

[189] Zakaria, op cit:26
[190] Anthony Davies, Will Iran Choose War?, Jane Defence Weekly, 23 September, 1998, Pg22
[191] Christopher Walker, Israel Helped India for 20 Years, The Times, Thursday June 4, 1998, Pg16
[192] Umer Farooq, Striking Consequences, Janes Defence Weekly, 2 September 1998, Pg23

Afghan refugees, ethnic tensions, drugs and the proliferation of small arms and also its high rates of poverty and illiteracy. However, tensions exist primarily with India and Pakistan and the future looks bleak, with numerous occasions where war has been imminent, usually over Kashmir. With the advanced military equipment incorporated into their respective armies and the acquisition of weapons of mass destruction (especially their nuclear capability), there is a serious risk of a nuclear war occurring between these two neighbours in the very near future.

I would like to remind the reader that this book is on Pakistan's perception of the threats it faces. It does not take into account the perception of other countries.

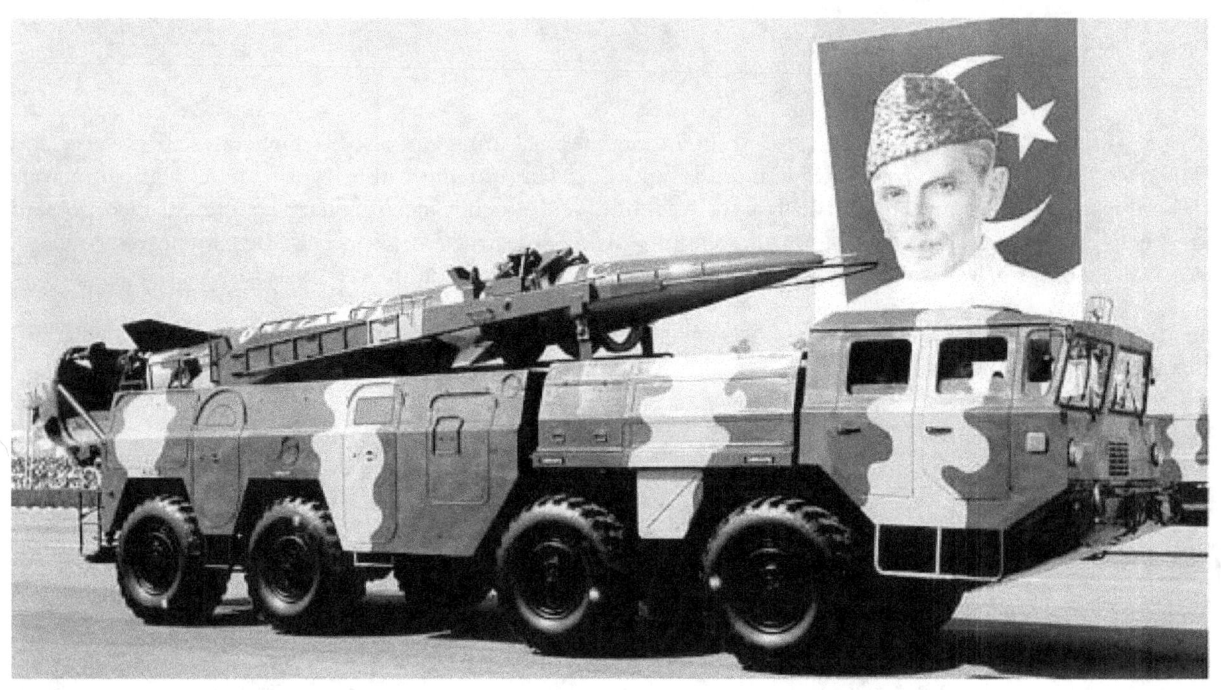

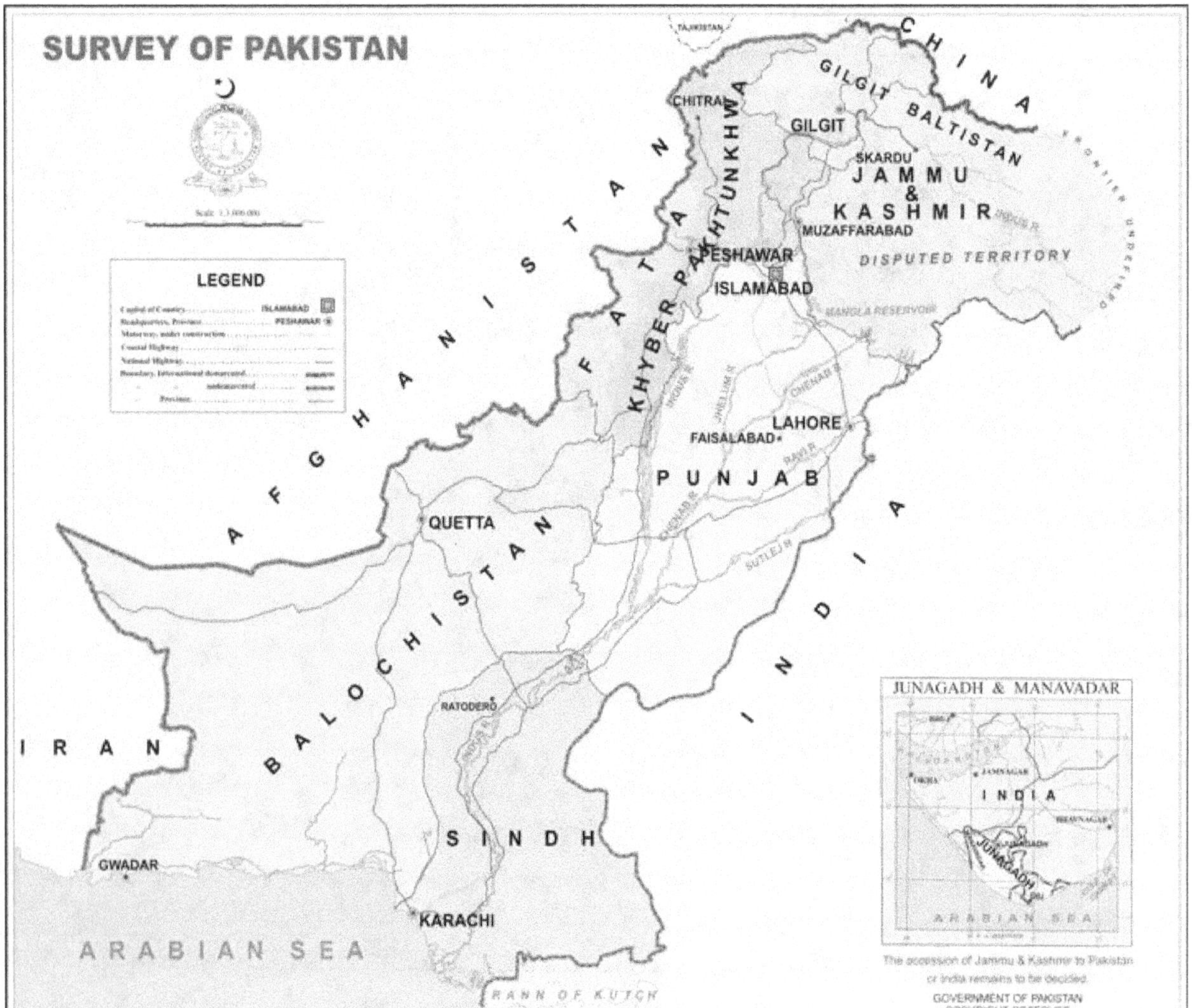
SURVEY OF PAKISTAN
LEGEND
TAJIKISTAN
CHINA
GILGIT BALTISTAN
CHITRAL
GILGIT
SKARDU
JAMMU & KASHMIR
MUZAFFARABAD
DISPUTED TERRITORY
FRONTIER UNDEFINED
PESHAWAR
ISLAMABAD
MANGLA RESERVOIR
KHYBER PAKHTUNKHWA
FATA
AFGHANISTAN
FAISALABAD
LAHORE
PUNJAB
QUETTA
BALOCHISTAN
INDIA
IRAN
RATODERO
SINDH
GWADAR
KARACHI
ARABIAN SEA
RANN OF KUTCH
JUNAGADH & MANAVADAR
INDIA
JUNAGADH
ARABIAN SEA
The accession of Jammu & Kashmir to Pakistan or India remains to be decided.
GOVERNMENT OF PAKISTAN
COPYRIGHT RESERVED

Pakistan Air Force Airborne Warning and Control System

M109 Paladin Howitzer Artillery

Pakistani Army Strategic Arsenal

Pakistan Army launches Operation Radd-ul-Fasaad to eliminate terrorism

References

Afzal Mahmood, Mini-Starwars in Asia?, Dawn publishers Ltd, 1998

Air Forces Monthly - http://www.airforcesmonthly.com/

Anthony Davies, Will Iran Choose War?, Jane Defence Weekly, 23 September 1998

Anthony H.Cordesman, Western Strategic Interests and the India-Pakistan Military Balance, Ian Allan Ltd, 1988

Arnett, Nuclear stability and arms sales to India, Arms Control Today, 1997

Ashok Kapur, Pakistan's attitude to the NPT, Parchment Press, 1993

Aviation Industry Chengdu Aircraft Industry (Group) Co., Ltd. - http://cac.avic.com/web/

Aviation Industry Corporation of China, Ltd. (AVIC) - http://www.avic.com/en/index.shtml?PC=PC

AVIC - http://www.avic.com/en/forbusiness/militaryaviationanddefense/fighters/394351.shtml

B.H.Farmer, An Introduction to South Asia, Richard Clay & Co.Ltd, 1983

Brassey's, World Aircraft & Systems Directory, Brassey's Ltd, 1996

C. Philips, The nuclear Casebook, Polygon Books, 1983

CAC/PAC JF-17 Thunder - https://en.wikipedia.org/wiki/CAC/PAC_JF-17_Thunder

CATIC - http://www.catic.cn/front

Chapter Six: Asia, 2018, The Military Balance, vol. 118, no. 1, pp. 219

Chapter six: Asia. (2017). *The Military Balance, 117*(1), 237-350.

Chinese Military Aviation - http://chinese-military-aviation.blogspot.co.uk/

Chris Bishop, Encyclopedia of Air Warfare-Volume 2, Aerospace Publishing Ltd, 1997

Chris Taylor, Military Balance in Southeast Asia, House of Commons Library, 2011

Christopher Walker and Michael Evans, Pakistan Feared Israeli Raid, The Times, Wednesday June 3, 1998

Christopher Walker, Israel's Helped India for 20 years, The Times, Thursday June 4, 1998

Cindy Shiner, International Herald Tribune, 1998

Combat Aircraft.Com - http://www.combataircraft.com/en/Military-Aircraft/Fighter-Attack/

David Albright and Tom Zamora, India and Pakistan go Nuclear, Bulletin of Atomic Scientists, 1989

David Axe, War Is Boring - https://medium.com/war-is-boring/this-is-the-ultimate-mig-21-715bb9297261

Dawn Weekly, Kashmir Policy, Touch Media Co.Ltd, 1998

Defence Industry Daily, Pakistan & China's JF-17 Fighter Program - https://www.defenseindustrydaily.com/stuck-in-sichuan-pakistani-jf17-program-grounded-02984/

Defence.pk - https://defence.pk/

Dreamstime - https://www.dreamstime.com/

Edward W.Desmond, Unity or Chaos?, Time, November 12, 1990

Eric Arnett, Delhi able to play nuclear trump in game for control of Kashmir, The Times, May 1998

Eric Arnett, Military Capacity and the Risk of War-China, India, Pakistan and Iran, Oxford University Press, 1997

Eric Arnett, What Threat?, Bulletin of the Atomic Scientists, 1997

Fareed Zakaria, How to be a Great Cheap, NewsWeek, T.P.L Printers Ltd, May 25, 1998

Flickr - https://www.flickr.com/search/?text=jf-17%20thunder

Flight Global - https://www.flightglobal.com/news/articles/nigeria-to-acquire-three-jf-17-fighters-444709/

Flight International, Airforces of the World Directory, Marketforce Ltd, 1998

General Walter Walker, The Next Domino?, The Covenant Publishing Co.Ltd, 1980

Global Security - https://www.globalsecurity.org/

Government of Pakistan, Ministry of Defence - http://www.mod.gov.pk/

Hafeez Malik, Dilemmas of National Security and Co-operation, The Macmillan Press Ltd, 1993

Ibid

IISS, Strategic Survey 2011 – The Annual Review of World Affairs, Routledge, 2011

IISS, Strategic Survey 2012 – The Annual Review of World Affairs, Routledge, 2012

IISS, Strategic Survey 2013 – The Annual Review of World Affairs, Routledge, 2013

Impact International, Delhi Expands its Strategic Swath, News & Media Ltd, 1996

Imtiaz Bakhari, The beginning of another 'Great Game'?, Jang Publishers Ltd, September 26, 1998

Indian Air Force - http://indianairforce.nic.in/

Indian Navy - https://www.indiannavy.nic.in/

Indian Army - https://indianarmy.nic.in/index.aspx

India Today, Future Fire, 1998

India Today, Games of Brinkmanship, 1987

India Today, India and Pakistan hours away from a nuclear war, 1994

India Today, India is now a nuclear weapon state, Living India Media Ltd, May 1998

India Today, India is now a Nuclear Weapon State, Living Media India Ltd, 1998

India Today, Pakistan's nuclear test, what now, June 1998

Inter Services Public Relations (ISPR) - https://www.ispr.gov.pk/

International Institute for Strategic Studies (IISS), Military Balance 1998-99, Oxford University Press, 1998

J.A.S Greenville, History of the World, HarperCollins Publishers, 1994

J.Goldstein & J. Pevehouse, International Relations, United States, 2007

Jane Nolan, Ballistic Missiles in the Third World, Brookings Institutions, 1991

Janes 360 - http://www.janes.com/article/search?query=+JF-17

Janes Defence Weekly (JDW), On the Line of Fire, Janes Information Group Ltd, 1998

JDW, A Loss of Momentum, 1997

JDW, A Loss of Momentum, 1997

JDW, Asia's Missile Race Hots Up, 1994

JDW, Asia's Missile Race Hots Up, 1994

JDW, Country Survey- Pakistan, 1992

JDW, Country Survey-India, 1990

JDW, Country Survey-Pakistan, 1992

JDW, Fighting on the Roof of the World, 1998

JDW, IAF Follows up on Su-30 Offer, 1994

JDW, India and Pakistan move to prevent nuclear disaster, March 1999

JDW, India becomes Sixth Nuclear Weapons State, 1998

JDW, India Budget May Affect Modernisation, 1998

JDW, India's Search for a New SPG, 1994

JDW, Indian Budget Fall May Affect Modernisation, 1998

JDW, Latest Tests put India in Nuclear Arms Spotlight, 1998

JDW, Mounting Tensions in South Asia, 1996

JDW, Nuclear Submarine is being built in India, December 1994

JDW, Pakistan Needs up to 70 Nuclear Warheads, June 1998

JDW, Pakistan's Time for Reassessment, 1998

JDW, Trials Provide Data for Range of Weapons Yields, 1998

JDW, USA links Chinese ties to missile Exports, 1994

JDW, Will Iran Choose War?, 1998

JF-17 Thunder - http://www.jf-17.com/

Johann Mcgeary, India's Surprise Nuclear Tests, Time May 25, 1998

Justin Bronk, So how good is Pakistan's JF-17 fighter? - https://hushkit.net/2018/01/25/so-how-good-is-pakistans-jf-17-fighter-analysis-from-rusi-think-tanks-justin-bronk/

KLJ-7A China Electronics Branch 14 airborne active phased array fire control radar - http://www.fx361.com/page/2017/0315/1131775.shtml

Lawrence Freedman, Atlas of Global Strategy, Macmillan Press Ltd, 1985

Lawrence Freedman, National Pride sets the Sabre Rattling, Daily Mail, May 29, 1998

Mahnaz Ipahani, Pakistan: dimensions of insecurity, Brassey's, 1990

Malcolm Chalmers, Confidence-Building in South-East Asia, Westview Press, 1996

Malcolm Chalmers, Owen Greene and Xie Zhiqiong, Asia Pacific Security & The UN, University of Bradford, 1995

Maleeha Lodhi, Nuclear Risk reduction and Conflict-Resolution in South Asia, Jang Publications Ltd, 1998

Mark J. Valencia, Trouble Waters, The Bulletin of the Atomic Scientists, 1997

Martin Sieff and Yoel Cohen, Pakistan Feared Israel's Strike during Nuclear test, Jewish Chronical, June 5 1998

Military Factory - https://www.militaryfactory.com/aircraft/detail.asp?aircraft_id=758

Military-Today.com - http://www.military-today.com/aircraft/jf17_thunder.htm

Ministry of Defence Production (Government Of Pakistan) - http://www.modp.gov.pk/

Ministry of Information Technology and Telecommunication (MoITT), Government of Pakistan - http://www.moit.gov.pk/

Mustaq Ali Khan, Pakistan Army Green Book, Ferozsons (Pvt) Ltd, 1990

News International, Advani's Nuclear Blackmail, August 10, 1998

News International, India will have to reclaim Azaad Kashmir says Defence Minister, Jang Publications Ltd, 1998

News International, Israel offers India AWACS for Airbases as Part of 'Common Threat Perception', Jang Publishers Ltd, April 18, 1995

News International, Nuclear arms not to be used: Nawaz, June 1998

Nick Bisley, Building Asia's Security, Routledge, 2009

Nils Bhinda, The Kashmir Conflict-1990, Earthscan Publication Ltd, 1994

Official Gateway To The Government Of Pakistan - http://www.pakistan.gov.pk/index.html

Pakistan Aeronautical Complex (PAC) - http://www.pac.org.pk/

Pakistan Air Force - http://www.paf.gov.pk/

Patrick Brogan, World Conflicts-Why and Where they are Happening, Bloomsbury Publishing Ltd, 1992

Paul Dibb, Towards a New Balance of Power in Asia, Adelphi Paper 295, Oxford University Press, 1995

Paul Rogers, Guide to Nuclear Weapons 1984-85, C.J.W Printers Ltd, 1984

Peter G. Tsourus, Changing Orders-The Evolution of the World's Armies, Arms and Armour Press, 1994

Pixabay
https://pixabay.com/en/photos/?q=military&image_type=&cat=&min_height=&min_width=&order=popular&pagi=2

Quwa Defence News & Analysis Group - https://quwa.org

Rahimullah Yusufzai, Taliban's Achilles Heels, Jang Publishers Ltd, November, 1998

Rockwell Collins - https://www.rockwellcollins.com

S.weibo.com - http://s.weibo.com/weibo/jf-17?topnav=1&wvr=6&b=1

Sean Kay, Global Security in the Twenty-First Century, Rowman & Littlefield Publishers, Inc, 2006

Senate Standing Committee on Defence and Defence Production - http://www.senatedefencecommittee.com.pk/

Sidney Bearman, Strategic Survey 1993-1994, Published by Brassey's for the IISS, 1994

SinoDefence.com (also known as "China Defence Today") - http://sinodefence.com/

Sohu FC-1 "Fierce Dragon" cockpit mystery - http://mil.sohu.com/20061102/n246145079_4.shtml

Stockholm International Peace Research Institute (SIPRI), World Military Expenditure Prices 1987-96, Oxford University Press, 1997

Sunday Telegraph, India Celebrates its Nuclear dream, May 1998

Tarun Basu, Selective Satellite Tracking of Missiles Alledged, India Abroad, 1997

The Daily Telegraph, Nuclear Blasts Puts Pakistan in Arms Race, 1998

The Diplomat - https://thediplomat.com/tag/jf-17-thunder/

The Economist, Asian Security, Published by the Economist Newspaper Ltd, 1996

The Military Balance, 01/2017, Volume 117, Issue 1

The News International, Armed to the Teeth, Jang Publishers Ltd, 1998

The Times, Pakistan Blasts into the Arms Race, Times Newspaper Ltd, 1998

Umer Farooq, Striking Consequences, Janes Defence Weekly, 2 September 1998

Venon Hewit, The New International Politics of South Asia, Manchester University Press, 1997

Walter Walker, The Next Domino?, The Covenant Publishing Ltd, 1980

Y. Ammar, The Kashmir Factor, Palestine Times, 9 October 1991

Yoel Cohen, India bomb test may affect Israel Relations, Jewish Cronicle, Publishers Jewish Chronical Newspaper Ltd, May 29, 1998

Zian Mian, No time to think, Jang Publishers Ltd, 1998

INDEX

The Pakistani COAS greeted soldiers on Eidul Azha in advance, while appreciating their morale, professionalism

ABOUT THE AUTHOR

Saghir Iqbal is a researcher in International Relations and Security Studies. He is an experienced Intelligence Analyst and has achieved a number of qualifications in this field. He is also a Lecturer in Business Management as well as an Examiner for A Level History and Business. Saghir Iqbal has a subject specialism in the following areas:

International Politics of the Cold War 1945-1991
Conflict Resolution in International Society+
Global and North-South Security Studies
Britain in the World
Disarmament Processes: History and Theory
Nationalism and Ethnicity in Post-Cold War Politics
Middle East: Area in Conflict
European Security
International Politics of the Environment
The United Nations, Peacekeeping and Intervention
Disarmament Processes: Current Problems
Globalisation and the South
International Terrorism
International Politics and Security Studies
Introduction to Peace Studies
Politics of the Global Environment
Regional Security in East Asia
Critical Security studies

Recently released books (2018)

- Dangerous Flashpoints in East Asia: The Military Build-up
- JF-17 Thunder: The Making of a Modern Cost- effective Multi-role Combat Aircraft
- Pakistan's War Machine: An Encyclopedia of its Weapons, Strategy and Military Security
- Miscalculation: Risks of Inadvertent Nuclear War

Website: www.saghir.co.uk